RESUMING MAURICE

GW00469595

'An altogether absorbing miscellany of literary biographical studies, shot through with wit and discernment. The flagship essay on Maeterlinck sets the standard, a brilliant elucidation of what made the writer so extraordinarily famous and bagged him the Nobel Prize for Literature before he more or less passes from popular consciousness. The linking theme with ten other essays, many of them gems, is the celebrity phenomenon, teasing out those mysterious properties which decide whether reputation is fugitive or permanent. Academic and recreational readers alike will acclaim Philip Mosley's own singular genius, the international sweep of his interests and understanding of people's vagaries. The autobiographical snippets deftly woven into every essay are a particular delight.'

Philip Waller, Emeritus Fellow of Merton College, Oxford, and author of
Writers, Readers, and Reputations: Literary Life in Britain 1870–1918 (2006)

In *Resuming Maurice*, Philip Mosley's brilliant collection of essays, not only do we learn how Maurice Maeterlinck managed his fame but how Karen Blixen's narcissism fed her writing and Dylan Thomas's star came to shine so brightly only to collapse. Readers are fascinated with context, and this volume offers tales of the well-known and the obscure in a most gratifying manner.

Bertha Rogers, Founding Director of Bright Hill Press, New York,
and translator of the letterpress edition of *Beowulf* (2000)

Resuming Maurice
And Other Essays on
Writers and Celebrity

Philip Mosley

Lasse Press

First published 2019
by the Lasse Press
2 St Giles Terrace, Norwich NR2 1NS, UK
www.lassepress.com
lassepress@gmail.com

ISBN-13: 978-1-9997752-6-1

Typeset in Garamond by
Curran Publishing Services Ltd, Norwich, UK

Manufactured in the UK by Imprint Digital, Exeter.

To Shu-ching

Contents

List of illustrations   viii
Preface   ix
Acknowledgements   xi

1   Resuming Maurice: Maeterlinck and literary celebrity   1

2   Out of Denmark: Karen Blixen   31

3   Review from the rectory: Whitwell Elwin   43

4   A cultivating pen: Vita Sackville-West   53

5   Modern romantics: Dylan Thomas and George Barker   61

6   A mightier pen: Ngugi wa Thiong'o   71

7   Roaring through life: John Seymour   79

8   Butterfly and tiger: Octavio Paz and Rosario Castellanos   87

9   A gentlewoman abroad: Virginia Haggard   97

10   Change and the modern churchman: J. K. Nettlefold   105

11   Waxing lyrical: Ned Washington   113

Index   123

Illustrations

Note: [p.d.] indicates a photo is understood to be now in the public domain. [WMC] indicates that the photographer has granted free use under the Creative Commons licence, and the work was sourced via Wikimedia Commons.

Frontispiece: the author, Schaarbeek, Brussels, 2013   xii
Maurice Maeterlinck photographed by Alvin Langdon Coburn, 1915 [p.d.]   2
Karen Blixen, Copenhagen Airport, 1957 [p.d.]   32
Jørgen Laursen Vig, Hesbjerg. Courtesy Frej Schmedes/from
   The Monastery: Mr. Vig and the Nun by Pernille Rose Grønkjær   39
Whitwell Elwin by Henry Weigall, RA, 1876. Photo Evelyn Simak [WMC]   42
Vita Sackville-West as a married woman [p.d.]   54
George Barker as a young man. Courtesy Elspeth Barker   60
Dylan Thomas photographed by Nora Summers, 1938. Courtesy
   Jeff Towns Dylan's Bookstore Collection   65
Ngugi wa Thiong'o, London, 2007. Photo: Sixoone [WMC]   70
John Seymour. Courtesy the Seymour family, www.pantryfields.com   80
Octavio Paz, Malmo Poetry Festival, 1988. Photo Jonn Leffmann [WMC]   91
Rosario Castellanos [p.d.]   95
Virginia Haggard writing. Courtesy Jean McNeil   96
J. K. Nettlefold on his graduation, 1921. Courtesy Winterbourne House
   and Garden   106
Ned Washington [p.d.]   112

Preface

Resuming Maurice is a collection of personal essays on greater and lesser known writers whose lives and careers have sparked some of my own literary and historical interests. Elements of personal narrative enter into my appreciations of this diverse set of authors and thinkers, whose backgrounds range from English (Vita Sackville-West, Whitwell Elwin, George Barker, John Seymour, Virginia Haggard, J. K. Nettlefold), Welsh (Dylan Thomas) and American (Ned Washington) to Belgian (Maurice Maeterlinck), Danish (Karen Blixen, Jørgen Laursen Vig), Mexican (Octavio Paz, Rosario Castellanos) and Kenyan (Ngugi wa Thiong'o). Corresponding to the growing academic subdiscipline of celebrity studies, a unifying theme of celebrity and its discontents runs throughout the volume. Additionally, my essays on Elwin, Barker, Seymour, and Nettlefold have an East Anglian connection in that these writers lived for part or all of their lives in a region of England where I was raised.

Philip Mosley
Clifton, Pennsylvania, February 2019

Acknowledgements

I am grateful to the following for their help, comments, and suggestions: Jean McNeil, Anne Sears, Philip Waller, Bertha Rogers, Charles Cantalupo, Sebastian Lockwood, Victoria Manthorpe, Andrew Gurr, Simon Lewis, Sevan Melikyan, Henrietta Lockhart, and Howard Hague.

An earlier version of 'Returning to Mr Vig' (the postscript to the chapter on Karen Blixen) was published in 'Connectivism', *Variety Crossing* (Canada) 13 (2011).

Thanks also to Susan Curran of Lasse Press for her enthusiastic support of this project.

The author, Schaarbeek, Brussels, 2013

1

Resuming Maurice:
Maeterlinck and literary celebrity

A pre-amble by way of reputation and renown

No matter how one chooses to define a literary celebrity, there is no doubt that Maurice Maeterlinck was one. For much of the first half of the twentieth century, the Nobel prizewinning Belgian was one of the most famous authors in the world, his books translated into many languages and selling in vast numbers. On his first visit to the United States in 1919, people clamoured to meet him and hear him speak. Bunting was hung in his honour along Fifth Avenue in New York City. Yet since his death in 1949 his oeuvre – poetry, plays, and essays – has been largely neglected. His translated works with few exceptions exist only in reprints of those that had poured from the printing presses in the first quarter of the century when he was at the peak of his fame.

Maeterlinck was rarely out of the public eye from the beginning of the century to the years before the Second World War, and enjoyed an exceptional span of literary celebrity. I mark this essay by several milestones in his career: 1890, when the playwright, novelist, and critic Octave Mirbeau hailed a 'new Shakespeare' on the publication of Maeterlinck's first play, *Princess Maleine*; 1901, when his nature essay *The Life of the Bee* created a global stir; 1908, when his play *The Blue Bird* began its extraordinary international popularity; 1911, when he won the Nobel Prize in Literature; and 1919 when, buoyed by his patriotic activities during the First World War, he took by storm first New York and then the rest of the United States. During that stay he became one of the earliest in a long line of émigré artists to hearken to the call of a Hollywood eager for European cultural valida-tion, though very little came of his brief arrangement with Samuel Goldwyn. The story goes that Goldwyn, on receiving a film treatment from Maeterlinck, rushed from his office shouting 'My God! My God! His hero is a bee!' The two scripts he completed never reached the screen.

Maeterlinck's reputation remained strong throughout the 1920s and 1930s, though he wrote less (and less well) in his later years. He signed off his career in Pascalian mode with a collection of childhood memories and other fragmentary reflections, *Blue Bubbles* (1948). The familiar 'public' discourse of his essays, which he couched in an elegant personal style, finally gave way to 'private' jottings, still worthy of a dedicated reader's attention but manifestly the work of a famous author ringing down the curtain (after all, he was a man of the theatre) on a long and distinguished career.

My own lengthy journey into the rich and strange spaces of francophone Belgian literature began in the dawning 1970s and resulted from several serendipitous connections. Robert Short, best known as an authority on surrealism, who taught in the sadly defunct School of European Studies at the University of East Anglia in Norwich, England, where I was a postgraduate student, put me in touch with the provocative Belgian underground film-maker Roland Lethem. On arriving in Belgium, I was unable to meet Lethem, but through him I found myself invited to a gathering of writers and artists in La Chambre des Imagiers, a *cercle privé* in a converted garage furnished with salvaged cinema seats in the Ixelles neighbourhood of Brussels. There I formed a lasting friendship with the poet Werner Lambersy and began to translate his work. My interest in francophone Belgian writing, an underrepresented and underestimated corpus in the history of European litera-ture, grew deeper and spurred me to translate Georges Rodenbach's 1892 novel *Bruges-la-Morte*. Nineteenth-century *fin de siècle* decadence was all the rage in the early 1970s. In turn, my discovery of Rodenbach's haunting novel led me to other francophone authors who belonged, as he had, to the socially ascendant Flemish bourgeoisie of that period. Among them notably were Emile Verhaeren and, *bien sûr*, Maurice Maeterlinck.

A later turn to ecocriticism in the literary world drew me to Maeterlinck's fame as a nature essayist, so I undertook a new translation of his 1907 essay *The Intel-ligence of Flowers*. He had achieved international literary celebrity on account of both his innovative Symbolist drama and the enormous success of his first major nature essay, *The Life of the Bee*. That since his lifetime he has been relatively forgotten prompted me subsequently to contemplate further the idea of celebrity and its discontents, as well as the vagaries of literary reputation.

By identifying celebrity with the construction of an image by or for an individual, Daniel Boorstin in 1963 was one of the first scholars to describe a major shift in Western culture away from the notion – traceable to Roman celebration of civic virtue – that fame and renown were rewards of accomplishment alone. Today, in a culture even more media-saturated than the one Boorstin described, when the line increas-ingly blurs between being a celebrity for what you have accomplished and being one for who you happen to be, it is unsurprising that celebrity studies has become a fully fledged academic subdiscipline with an eponymous journal and a corresponding round of international conferences. An offshoot of cultural studies, its main interest is in contemporary celebrity, but it has also begun historicizing the phenomenon as well as exploring more complex distinctions: for instance, that between celebrity and charisma, the latter being perceived as a facet of personality alone.

Celebrity may have originated in the medieval Christian cult of the saints. As a modern literary phenomenon, it has been identified with Enlightenment figures such as Voltaire and Samuel Johnson. In the anglophone context, at least, it emerged more clearly in the Romantic period (Tom Mole's 2007 study of Byron, for instance, contends that even he felt the burden of public expectation), gathered pace during the nineteenth century (as in the cases of Charles Dickens, Benjamin Disraeli, Alfred Tennyson, and Mark Twain), and evolved to the point of producing a figure such as Maeterlinck (in the French-speaking world) by the beginning of the twentieth century. Philosophically, its starting point was a post-Rousseau cult of subjectivity; socio-economically, it depended on a commercialized literary system forged by the growing industrial production of books, newspapers, and magazines.

This mass production depended equally on technological advances: the rotary press, for instance, was invented in 1812. The upshot was a sea change in literary culture which brought with it an increasing number of critics, reviewers, and readers (due also in no small measure to the extension of education), an audience for public events such as lecture tours, and a wide dissemination of related visual images made possible by the rapidly developing art of photography.

By the time of Maeterlinck's career as an author (loosely 1890 to 1940), a literary star system was fully in place, fed by fan mailers, tourists, autograph hunters, journalists, publishers, agents, trustees, executors, memoirists, and assorted other players. The rise of academic literary studies and the corresponding construction of a canon of major authors and texts also played their parts. The term 'best seller' is an American coinage from 1889. We may add to this cumulative process the elaborate promotion and publicity of writing and writers via motion pictures and then radio – all bolstered by emerging modern techniques of advertising, marketing, and public relations.

These combined elements gave rise to a modern idea of celebrity in which the fame of an author was deftly and systematically mediated by agents, by commercial cultural producers, and not least by authors themselves. In *Intimate Strangers: The Culture of Celebrity* (1985), Richard Schickel points out that George Gissing's novel *New Grub Street* (1891) was the old street of literary hacks freshly commodified: the future belonged to the Jasper Milvains of this world. Thus, by 1925, writers and readers alike had the press, radio, and cinema at their disposal. Mole describes this audience as 'massive, anonymous, socially diverse and geographically distributed'. A mutual negotiation of literary celebrity had taken definite shape.

To retain the status of literary celebrity depends upon the vagaries of literary reputation, and such reputations are inherently unpredictable and unstable phenomena. They may rise and fall for specific reasons and occasionally for no clear reason at all.

What is clear is that they answer to vogues in literary taste and criticism, to notions of political correctness, to demands of the marketplace whether driven by publisher or reader, to cultural zeitgeists, to perceptions of the author's life and personality, and to zealous missions of rehabilitation whether ideologically or emotionally driven, or both, and those often on the part of other authors. It was not until the 1930s, by which time he had been dead for over forty years, that Herman Melville's literary greatness was recognized. It was not that he had garnered much of a reputation in his lifetime. Driven into isolation by the stony and uncomprehending reception of complex early works like *Mardi*, *Pierre*, and *Moby Dick*, he was all but forgotten; in 1891, the august *New York Times* obituary referred to him as 'Henry' Melville.

More recently, among crusading fellow authors, few have shown greater zeal than Alice Walker, whom I picture one hot day in the early 1970s scouring the dry corners of a Florida field, pushing back tall weeds in search of Zora Neale Hurston's grave. She found it, of course, and her influential 1975 article 'Looking for Zora' in *Ms.* magazine was the impetus to Hurston's renewed reputation. An unjustly forgotten figure from the Harlem Renaissance thus finally got her due. Walker may have set a postmodern trend of revisiting ignored or misunderstood artists: witness the recurring words 'looking for', 'searching for', 'finding', and 'becoming' in contemporary titles of this kind.

❀❀❀

In this recuperative spirit, I am here 'resuming Maurice'; that is to say, I am both essaying an embroidered resumé of Maeterlinck's celebrated literary career and encouraging a recovery, or a resumption, of his reputation. I 'resume' an author whose work in one genre, that of drama, represents a significant part of the transition from nineteenth-century Romanticism to the modernism of the early twentieth century, and in another genre, that of the popular essay, offers a curious resistance to that change.

Though Maeterlinck was less reclusive than, for instance, J. D. Salinger or Thomas Pynchon, he belongs alongside them as a reluctant celebrity – in stark contrast to, say, F. Scott Fitzgerald, Ernest Hemingway, and Norman Mailer, all of whom came after him. In thinking of such American writers, we may duly observe that the tension Maeterlinck felt between his identity as a serious writer and as an object of popular adulation was exacerbated by his transatlantic experience. Loren Glass (*Authors Inc.*, 2004) and Leo Braudy (*The Frenzy of Renown*, 1997), among others, have distinguished between a European elitism firmly wedded to the idea of artistic detachment and an American populism geared to a voracious celebrity culture and a relentless marketing of books. While this continental distinction no longer holds good today in a ubiquitous celebrity culture driven by advanced mass media, it did so for the most part in a modernist era that encompassed the career of the traditionalist Maeterlinck, at a time when the relationship between author and reader generally still valued a measure of distance and decorum over an unfettered intimacy and obsession.

Describing a 'tension between impersonality and personality', Glass examines the case of Gertrude Stein, for so long a European exile from her native land, and an author whose paradoxical celebrity bears useful comparison with that of Maeterlinck. Glass invokes Pierre Bourdieu's contrast between an 'autonomous' literary culture in which the modernist author operates within a restricted avant-garde milieu and a 'heteronomous' culture of accessible literary texts whose mass marketing is backed up by a highly visible author. With the 1933 publication of *The Autobiography of Alice B. Toklas*, Stein forsook her exclusive formalism for a more conventional work that perfectly framed her American return as a popular writer, with its attendant public appearances and a 1934 lecture tour. In search of the recognition she believed she deserved, the 'European' Stein had reinvented herself as a popular 'American' author, if not exactly as a prodigal American daughter. And while her stock (in more than one sense) rose in the United States on the strength of her newly willed inclusivity, it fell equally sharply among the intellectual elite of Europe, for whom exclusivity was all. Moreover, it left Stein famous but unsure of her own identity as an author, as *Everybody's Autobiography* (1937) often painfully reveals.

Stein had followed in the footsteps of Maeterlinck. He had first arrived in the United States fifteen years earlier to great acclaim as a serious European writer and thinker, who nonetheless had the common touch both in his popular essay style and in having written a play, *The Blue Bird*, that appealed to all age groups and intellectual levels. If ever an author understood how to reach the common reader consistently, then it was Maeterlinck. By comparison, Stein's populist moment was a brief, one-off affair.

According to Braudy, the cultural life of the nineteenth century had generated a tension between assertion and evasion. A 'posture of reticence' traceable back to Byron represents the post-Romantic author's desire to nurture and maintain artistic integrity via a careful strategy of hiding in broad daylight, of combining an enviable isolation from the public with a shrewd handling of financial and cultural currencies. Celebrity studies have begun to explore, as Lorraine York puts it, 'a production of reluctance for promotional purposes', in which an author simultaneously accepts and rejects the construction of a public image. In his 2006 book *Writers, Readers, and Reputations: Literary Life in Britain, 1870–1918*, Philip Waller observes that both Joseph Conrad and Henry James, though outwardly scornful of literary commerce, presented themselves readily for reproducible portraiture in several visual forms.

From Maeterlinck's early days as a reluctant young lawyer with eyes turned to Paris, poetry – a volume of Symbolist poems, *Hothouses* (1889), was his first published work – and then plays, on through his remarkable rise to fame, and even into his less illustrious later years as a grey eminence of European literature, he remained a detached individual, sparing of words, desirous of solitude and silence, and never feeling at ease with public life and the endless calls upon him to participate in it.

Like other famous writers of his time – Arthur Conan Doyle, George Bernard Shaw, and H. G. Wells come to mind – Maeterlinck was a strong, athletic man, keen on sports and outdoor activities such as boxing, fencing, weightlifting, fishing, bicycling, gardening, and boating. He was known to roller-skate from one end to the other of his sprawling home in the Norman abbey of St Wandrille. Yet he was a shy, sensitive, and nervous soul, who sought a balance between the physical and the mental life in the welcome seclusion of his country houses or in the strict privacy of his villas on the French Riviera.

His gregarious and opportunistic partner, the French actress Georgette Leblanc, sustained and largely directed his fame and reputation for more than twenty years. That was at least Leblanc's own view in her waspish 1928 *Souvenirs* of life with the 'lion', a set of largely unflattering reminiscences that succeeded in driving Maeterlinck back into his natural shell. His diffident celebrity was accentuated by his discomfort in public speaking, even more so when not in his native French, and in enduring the small-talking, glad-handing motions that his popularity demanded of him.

According to his friend, the Flemish author Cyriel Buysse, Maeterlinck rarely engaged in literary discussion, preferring to ride his bicycle, walk his dog, smoke his pipe, and (like Rudyard Kipling, also an enthusiast of this new mode of transport) drive the Daimler car that fame had placed in his driveway in return for a company endorsement. His reluctant celebrity may have eventually taken a toll on his writing. We are reminded of Hemingway, who in his 1959 Nobel acceptance speech remarked that loneliness goes away with the gaining of greater stature, but the work often suffers as a result. Like Maeterlinck, he chose not to attend the prizegiving ceremony.

In any age, there are authors who revel in the limelight, unable to get enough of their eager, adoring followers. Equally, there are those who shun the stage on which their celebrity plays out, one spotlighted and overcrowded with long lines of readers waving books to be signed, with journalists and critics sharpening their pencils to a fine point of praise or dismissal, with photographers seeking the next photo-op, and with social and political movers, shakers, and general hangers-on always looking for the right opportunity to invest in some promising cultural capital. Maeterlinck belongs to this second type of author, one that fits perfectly the myth of the European artist-intellectual prevalent since the Romantics: Shelley's 'unacknowledged legislator', an author of and often for the people, but superbly (in more than one French sense of this word) detached from them.

Given the increasing interpenetration of the cultural and the economic, says Glass, 'literary celebrity as a historically specific articulation of the dialectical tension between modern consciousness and public subjectivity persists only as a residual model of authorship'. Put less theoretically, the culture to which Maeterlinck belonged has gone for good, the one that gave rise, at least in continental Europe if less so in the United Kingdom and the United States, to the successful and acclaimed author standing at a dignified and almost expected remove from his public. Braudy maintains that after the Civil War the American image ceded its noble, restrained European sheen to the individual exploitation of the 'theater of public life'. In the American tradition, this cultivated public image has long been a vital part of the literary enterprise. Twain began it, Jack London bought into it, as later also did Stein and Hemingway, albeit in a highly conflicted manner, and Mailer thrived on it. Self-promotion and public visibility have increasingly corresponded to the idea of a club of one's peers, to a place on the bestseller list, to a space in the reviewer's column, and to a seat in the interviewee's chair. By the 'pop' 1960s, a direct engagement with one's readers was perceived as normal practice, and one to be actively encouraged.

In 1965, in the *New York Times*, Kurt Vonnegut wryly described Tom Wolfe's *The Kandy-Kolored Tangerine-Flake Streamline Baby* as an 'excellent book by a genius who will do anything to get attention'. This level of postmodern irony is possible only among those of genuine literary distinction; the present consensus thus allows Dave Eggers his tongue-in-cheek novelistic title *A Heartbreaking Work of Staggering Genius*. But recognizable talent no longer stops run-of-the-mill writers from jumping on the bandwagon of promiscuous self-advertisement. One no longer needs to be anointed either by critics or by one's peers. Any author – good, bad, or indifferent – may advertise and advocate his or her talent via the internet: blogs, web sites, Facebook pages, etc., ad infinitum, ad absurdum, ad nauseam. In his 2007 nove*l Exit Ghost*, Philip Roth gives his alter ego Nathan Zuckerman his last stand for the ravaged values of traditional literary culture. That William Faulkner should be ignored while mediocre, politically correct writers are welcomed and even adulated drives Zuckerman to fits of apoplexy. We may understand his rage.

Authors who shun the public eye are viewed now as curious eccentrics, if strangely newsworthy for that very reason. In an overheated celebrity culture, even the holdouts gain notoriety for stances that some ultimately cannot maintain. Such recluses have become the stuff of legend: Salinger, the earlier William Gaddis, Pynchon (until his voiceover cameo on *The Simpsons*), and Cormac McCarthy (until he appeared on the *Oprah Winfrey Show*). And there seems little doubt that Harper Lee – despite her closeness to Truman Capote, who was hardly a shrinking violet – was pushed back reluctantly into the limelight with the publication of *Go Set a Watchman*, her 'rediscovered' (though long shelved by her) sequel to her masterpiece *To Kill a Mockingbird*.

Maeterlinck, however, was not a recluse by the extreme standards of those individuals. Though he disliked publicity and preferred to avoid the crowds, he usually went along as good-naturedly as possible with the expectation that he would have to go on periodic show as a world-famous author. In France he could retreat to his private homes and so minimize his exposure, but abroad in countries such as Italy, England, and the United States it was well-nigh impossible for him to escape close attention. Nonetheless, he understood the importance of the burgeoning mass media to his own career and to his audience, and so was not entirely averse to their functions or blind to their possibilities. In a way, he had his cake and ate it too, since he enjoyed his international status as a consummate popularizer, in his essay collections, of difficult and often nebulous ideas in philosophy, science, and art. That he wore his mantle with a degree of hauteur was by and large expected of him as a literary sage in the French intellectual mould, one who occasionally descended from his ivory tower to meet those ordinary folks waiting on his every word. For the most part he kept a polite distance, a laconic style of speech, and an inscrutable expression, as befitted a man whom his biographer and friend Patrick Mahony described as 'the first important literary mystic in the modern world'.

August 1890: Mirbeau hails a 'new Shakespeare'

Writing in the newspaper *Le Figaro* on 24 August 1890, Octave Mirbeau praised Maeterlinck's first play, *Princess Maleine*, as 'the most brilliant, extraordinary and also naïve work of our time, comparable, and – dare I say it? – superior in beauty to that which is most beautiful in Shakespeare' (including *Hamlet* and *Macbeth*).

Mirbeau, who also wrote plays and naturalist novels, belonged to a dwindling tradition of author-journalists in the days before criticism fell mainly into the hands of professional academics. The pioneering critic René Wellek points out, for instance, that Matthew Arnold may have held the Oxford chair in poetry from 1857, but most of his criticism was written for periodicals. Nineteenth-century literary criticism flourished in daily papers, weeklies, monthlies, and quarterlies. Though the quarterlies were serious forums for the literati and the more frequent publications appealed to a growing middle-class readership, it was in these various versions of the press that reviewers exercised their power and influence.

At 28 and hitherto little known in France, Maeterlinck awoke famous (in the Byronic sense) on the morning of 25 August 1890. Mirbeau had singlehandedly blazed his trail to critical renown. Meanwhile, across the English Channel, an article entitled 'A new Shakespeare' appeared in the *Manchester Guardian* on 28 October 1890. The ripple effect of Mirbeau's eulogy spread rapidly to Germany, Austria, and elsewhere in Europe.

Besides offering a rigourous intellectual training, one has to wonder what those Jesuit fathers put in the drinking water at the Collège Sainte-Barbe in Ghent. By 1874, when 12-year-old Maeterlinck enrolled as a pupil in that austere *lycée*, it had already produced two important literary figures-to-be, Rodenbach and Verhaeren. Moreover, the poet and short story writer Grégoire Le Roy was Maeterlinck's classmate, while poet and playwright Charles Van Lerberghe joined them in the following year. During Maeterlinck's time at the college, however, there was little to suggest that an unusually talented author was in the making, despite a friendship among these three young men that cemented itself in 1879 toward the end of their school days. The laconic Maeterlinck contrasted with the extroverted Le Roy, while the former wrote disparagingly of his own prowess as a pupil, and of the school where he endured a mostly wretched existence.

Privately reluctant but acceding to his family's wishes, Maeterlinck entered the University of Ghent to study law. By this time, the trio of friends were already more interested in literature. In 1881, they duly subscribed to the magazine *La Jeune Belgique*, the flagship publication for the idea of a distinctive Belgian component of French literature. In 1883, Maeterlinck attended a noted banquet in honour of his compatriot Camille Lemonnier, an event that pressed the Belgian literary project forward. In the same year, Maeterlinck (under the pseudonym of M. Mater) published his first poem, 'In the rushes', in *La Jeune Belgique*. But there was little response to this poem or to other efforts to publish his work. In 1884 Max Waller, the editor of the magazine, rejected one of Maeterlinck's efforts dedicated to Van Lerberghe as 'bad, extremely bad'. Undeterred by these setbacks, he pursued his law degree while immersing himself in literature on every available occasion.

In late 1885, he and Le Roy went to Paris, Maeterlinck ostensibly to familiarize himself with court procedure and oratory. Their true intent, though, was to discover other writers by frequenting the capital's restaurants and bars. In the Brasserie Pousset they met Villiers de l'Isle-Adam, who was busy turning his back on outmoded realism and embracing fully the delights of Symbolism. Villiers quickly won over Maeterlinck and his confrères, who were further encouraged by Rodenbach's acknowledgement of them; he described Maeterlinck as a 'truly Flemish mind with undertones of dreams and their sensitivity to colour. Deep down, a silent one, who doesn't easily give of himself.' Maeterlinck's taciturnity surely appealed to Rodenbach, who built his entire career around an aesthetic of silence embodied by Beguine nuns and graceful swans gliding along the deserted quays and equally grey canals of his beloved and timeless Bruges.

Still lukewarm about practising law and now dreaming of isolating himself in the countryside, Maeterlinck collected together some of the poems he had published in magazines to form his first book, *Hothouses*. Though these poems, which he dismissed later as insignificant juvenilia, have been reassessed favourably today, they were completely lost in the shuffle that occurred the following August, when Mirbeau hailed the young author instead for his promise in the dramatic arts.

Maeterlinck's explosion onto the literary scene was all the more remarkable for its unexpectedness. In 1889, at the author's own cost, his Ghent friend Louis Van Melle printed a mere thirty copies of *Princess Maleine* with a frontispiece by the Bruges artist Georges Minne, which Maeterlinck distributed to his friends and to various Parisian acquaintances. The story goes that one copy reached Stéphane Mallarmé, hardly the wrong person to have read your work approvingly, who passed it to Mirbeau, probably expecting him to give it a good but minor notice.

We see here the importance of personal connection. Similarly, the poet Stefan George later discovered Verhaeren by word of mouth, and was responsible for establishing the Belgian poet's strong German reputation.

Princess Maleine was first published commercially in 1890 in a limited print run by Paul Lacomblez in Brussels, and reprinted in the wake of Mirbeau's review in a much larger number. The play was also published in serial form in the review *La Société Nouvelle*, and was followed later in 1890 by *The Intruder*, also praised by Mirbeau, and *The Blind*. In the space of a few months, the young poet-in-waiting had been transformed into the hottest new playwright in the French language.

As for a stage production, Maeterlinck offered *Princess Maleine* to the avowedly experimental hand of André Antoine at the Théâtre Libre, and while Antoine prevaricated, Maeterlinck turned down a request for it by Paul Fort at the Théâtre d'Art. Incredibly it remained unstaged in France until 1962. Fort did produce the less acclaimed *The Blind* at the Théâtre d'Art in 1891, and the same company staged *The Intruder* at the Vaudeville in a production by Aurélien Lugné-Poe.

Hard on the heels of the first three plays, *The Seven Princesses* was published in 1891, though Maeterlinck was sufficiently disappointed in it to leave it out of his 1901–02 three-volume *Theatre* collection. Meanwhile, the career of the future mass-market mystic was forming in his translation of *The Adornment of the Spiritual Marriage* by the fourteenth-century Dutch mystic Jan van Ruusbroec, a text that had deeply moved the young author in a way that the works of Novalis and Ralph Waldo Emerson would also do.

The first signs of Maeterlinck's resistance to his sudden celebrity lay in his refusal in 1891 of both the triennial drama prize and the quinquennial literary prize offered by the Belgian Royal Academy. These declinations set the tone for much of his long career, one marked by a consistent aversion to the bestowing upon him of honours and awards. We may understand his not refusing the Nobel in 1911, but he proved disinclined even to celebrate that ultimate achievement.

With the Symbolist movement in literature reaching its apogee in the fin de siècle, Maeterlinck's plays stood as its exemplary dramatic representation. Atmosphere, interiority, allusion, immobility, and silence pervade them. Defining his drama as 'the tragedy of the everyday', Maeterlinck wrote one eerie, 'static' play after another. Their author was hailed for his Symbolist vagueness and ethereality; also as a pioneering technician of a new kind of drama that challenged both the limitations of naturalism and the tired conventions of social comedy and boulevard vulgarity, then stunting the evolution of theatre in France.

Amid a welter of productions in France, Belgium, and elsewhere, Maeterlinck continued to feed a seemingly insatiable appetite for his dramas of inaction, or at least of an indirect form of action framed by medieval legend and lore. *Pelleas and Melisande* appeared in 1892, though it did not get its full due until controversially set as an opera to Claude Debussy's music in 1901. Even so, the Parisian premiere of the play was a notable event, not least for its being produced in May 1893 by

Maurice Maeterlinck photographed by Alvin Langdon Coburn, 1915

Lugné-Poe for the Théâtre Libre at the Bouffes-Parisiens, a vaudeville house by night featuring a show enticingly entitled *Madame Suzette*. Founded in 1887 on a shoestring by Paris Gas Company employees and theatre lover André Antoine, the Théâtre Libre soon became the go-to company in Paris for experimental and iconoclastic plays. Forced out of business by mounting debts in 1894, Antoine saw his company survive until 1896, and was able to look back on a decade of nose-thumbing in the face of a palsied, predictable, and unimaginative French theatrical scene.

Maeterlinck declined to take a bow at the *Pelleas and Melisande* premiere, as he had done two years earlier by having failed to show up to the premiere of *The Intruder*. Befitting his dislike of public performance, he would have preferred his plays to exist purely as dramatic literature rather than as theatrical spectacles. This preference lay too in his belief that Symbolist drama depended for its meaning and effect on language rather than action. Yet, as he argued in 'Silence' and 'The tragic in everyday life', two essays in the volume *The Treasure of the Humble* (1896), even language itself is suspect; 'unsaid' dialogue counts for as much as that which is spoken. Furthermore, he had no time for acting, and believed that it interfered with the resonance of his symbolic language. The actor was his 'intruder'; in an issue of *La Jeune Belgique*, he wrote that 'something of Hamlet is dead to us on the very day when we have seen him die onstage. The appearance of an actor has ousted him, and we can no longer dismiss the usurper of our dreams.'

The Seven Princesses was first performed privately by puppets in 1892, so it is unsurprising that Maeterlinck came up in 1894 with three 'plays for marionettes': *Alladine and Palomides, Interior,* and *The Death of Tintagalies.* The word 'interior' was by then almost a trademark of his plays, while the mysterious archaism of his protagonists' names made clear that such drama was far removed from the realism or social mannerism of the present day. The presence of death in life, the sacrifice of purity and innocence – yet with an overarching sense of a great and wonderful secret always just beyond our reach – mark all of Maeterlinck's early plays. Writing to Verhaeren in late 1891, Maeterlinck described *The Intruder, The Blind,* and *The Seven Princesses* as 'a little trilogy of death'. And the subsequent marionette trilogy offered more of the usual suspense and stripped-down language. *Alladine and Palomides* and *The Death of Tintagilies* were very popular in England, *Interior* more so in France. *Alladine* was a mini-version of *Pelleas and Melisande*, with tragic lovers in the Tristan and Iseult/Romeo and Juliet tradition. *Tintagilies* involves the murder of a child, while *Interior* harks back to *The Intruder*, though its characters stay speechless throughout; creeping death viewed from the outside in.

Maeterlinck's Symbolist plays bear reconsidering today both for their conceptual daring, which remains the key to their dramaturgical quality, and for the way in which they anticipate the modern theatre of alienation in which characters act or react helplessly, ludicrously, or desperately to forces they cannot understand or control. We might find it hard to imagine the drama of Samuel Beckett, Eugene Ionesco, Jean-Paul Sartre, Albert Camus, and Harold Pinter – to name but several major figures – without recalling the claustrophobic settings and the isolated, anxiety-ridden characters of Maeterlinck's plays. And these shadowy, Kafkaesque situations bordering on the absurd still answer to the restlessness and paranoia of our postmodern world with its virtual realities, fragmentary modes of communication, governmental and corporate doubletalk, and bewildering internet babble.

Moreover, the pseudo-historical, legendary settings of Maeterlinck's plays would seem to strike a chord with present devotees of popular fantasy fiction and video games, both of which are suffused with medieval names and places, peopled by aristocrats and royalty, by evil tyrants and star-crossed lovers, all set against looming castles, dark forests, and even darker interiors. His plays are redolent of Thomas Malory, whose work he admired as much as the children's books of his own time illustrated by such English artists as Randolph Caldecott, Kate Greenaway, and Walter Crane. Maeterlinck also worked on book illustration, costume and stage design with Symbolist and Post-Impressionist artists like George Minne, Georges de Feure, and Edouard Vuillard, as well as with the American photographer Alvin Langdon Coburn, whose portrait of the author graces this essay.

Adapting John Ford's Jacobean incest tragedy *'Tis Pity She's a Whore* as *Annabella* in 1895, Maeterlinck saw an affinity between his despairing scenarios and Ford's own interest in doomed lovers caught in psychosexual fixes and in atmospheres inspired by Ford's contemporary Robert Burton's treatise *Anatomy of Melancholy*. We may observe two other factors shaping Maeterlinck's celebrity in 1895. He translated *The Disciples at Saïs* and *Fragments* by Novalis, so furthering his interest in a romantic mysticism which in his own essays would boost his readership greatly. He also met Georgette Leblanc, with whom he enjoyed a twenty-three-year liaison, and who energetically encouraged and promoted his international career in a manner that would have been unlikely had he been left to his own devices. Their partnership would end painfully in 1918; soon thereafter, Maeterlinck married another young actress, Renée Dahon, whom he had known since she had played in *The Blue Bird* in Paris in 1911. The final split between Maeterlinck and Georgette led eventually to the discomfiting revelations in her *Souvenirs*.

During the final five years of the nineteenth century, apart from a brief and later disowned return to poetry resulting in *Twelve Songs* (1896, expanded to fifteen songs in a 1900 edition), Maeterlinck turned his attention to the essay, which proved to be a perfect vehicle for the lucid and fluent expression of his post-Romantic spiritual vision and of its moral, social, and scientific implications. His first essay collection, *The Treasure of the Humble* (1896), went through seven editions in that year alone, and caused almost as much of a stir as had his early plays. Translated into English in 1897, it sold 8,000 copies in one year, and 40,000 more in the years leading up to the First World War. Meanwhile, other than for the tragic love triangle portrayed in *Aglavaine and Selysette* (1896), Maeterlinck's work in Symbolist drama was complete, forming a dense oeuvre that epitomized the rise of a modern European theatre to match the achievements in poetry of Mallarmé, Paul Verlaine, and Arthur Rimbaud.

It soon became clear to Georgette, if less pressingly to Maeterlinck, that he should move from Ghent to Paris. In the spring of 1897 they took an apartment there, one they kept until acquiring a large Italianate villa in Passy in 1900. Doubtless with Georgette orchestrating the move, it seemed to announce the definite metropolitan establishment of an author whose address now matched his ever-growing reputation. They continued to summer in the Normandy country-side, and during one long bicycle ride in 1897 discovered a former presbytery in

Gruchet-Saint-Siméon which they promptly rented. In doing so, they followed an urban–rural, winter–summer pattern which Maeterlinck had enjoyed in his youth on Boulevard Frère-Orban in Ghent and at his family's country house in Oostaker to the north of the city. The presbytery was the first of a number of houses of various sizes in which Maeterlinck would make his home. He would oscillate between city and country, between a reluctant visibility (if not on Georgette's part) and a desired invisibility, between a public presence and a private absence, a set of binaries that would drive the tense dialectic of his literary fame.

The Treasure of the Humble offered a pessimistic view of human life, consistent with the mood of Maeterlinck's plays, but his second essay collection, *Wisdom and Destiny* (1898), revealed a very different side of the author in its cheerful, more optimistic tone. He made the case for a stoical moralism, for a responsibility to others, for compassion, justice, and the perfection of ordinary life. It was the early sign of a transformed outlook on body, soul, and world, which would last for fifteen years during the height of his fame, and mark both his essay writing and a triumphantly renewed dramatic output. Georgette felt she could take much of the credit for Maeterlinck's change of heart, and did so to the extent of claiming co-authorship of *Wisdom and Destiny.* He gently deflected her claim in his dedication of the volume: 'It has been enough that my eyes have followed you closely in life, that in that they thus followed the movements, gestures and habits of wisdom itself.' The intellectual and emotional shift revealed by the volume did not disturb Maeterlinck's readers at all. Published simultaneously in London, Paris, and New York, and in a French edition that sold 100,000 copies over a thirty-year period, it proved as successful as its predecessor, and suggested that followers of his essays were in thrall as much to his verbal charm and communicative skill as to the tenor of his philosophical speculations.

As a new century beckoned, Maeterlinck immersed himself in entomological research. He was always an eager naturalist ready to take country walks or potter in his garden, and his rental of the Gruchet presbytery aided his investigations. The retreat offered him and Georgette a welcome escape from the hurly-burly of Parisian social life. He rediscovered the pioneering ten-volume late-nineteenth-century work on insects by Jean-Henri Fabre, whose undoubted expertise was compromised only by a singular lack of style. Maeterlinck decided to compensate for Fabre's literary weakness by spending the years 1899 and 1900 researching and drafting his own essay on bees; it became *The Life of the Bee.* This volume formed the first of his four great nature essays, and catapulted him into an early twentieth-century version of literary superstardom. Some irony resides in Maeterlinck later being invited, on the strength of his own book, to write a preface to a 1910 work on spiders by none other than Fabre.

Regarding the French reception of Maeterlinck's early work, we may note that despite Mirbeau's encomium and praise from other critics, his plays met with reservations in various quarters. The dogged defence of social mannerism (in the works of Emile Augier and Alexandre Dumas, fils), of historical drama (Victorien Sardou), and of comic grotesquerie (Georges Courteline) by professional critics such as Paul Adam and Francisque Sarcey, the latter the anointed king of Parisian drama reviewers, left little or no room for the innovations of naturalist playwrights like Henry Becque or Symbolists like Maeterlinck. The reasons for this resistance to Maeterlinck and his work are many. Some were born of nationalistic pride, others of plain aesthetic conservatism; sometimes they were a hard-headed mélange of the two.

To these adversaries Maeterlinck was neither French nor 'southern' but Belgian – and Flemish or 'northern' to boot – and so, by way of a perverse logic, almost certainly a dangerous Germanophile, contrary in thought and expression to the French mind, whatever that idea may have been taken to mean at the time. Mirbeau, even he, carefully avoided identifying Maeterlinck's origin in his paean to *Princess Maleine*: 'I don't know where he's from.' Others perceived Maeterlinck as a plagiarist of French literature, a rank outsider pretending to an inconceivable command of the French language and its modes of expression. Put simply, they saw him as threatening the sanctity of the French tradition. Critics whose sense of francophone culture stopped at the hexagonal border conveniently ignored the fact that no young French author seemed able to match his early accomplishments.

In the minds of nationalists gathering around Charles Maurras and his Action française group or adhering to the early boulangiste patriotism of Maurice Barrès, for an individual to be foreign regardless of native language meant nothing less than ineligibility for a significant role in advancing French culture. Maeterlinck's nationality rendered him suspect in the eyes of those for whom Belgium was a pro-German nation. King Leopold II was not only an imperialistic rogue, as his adventures in the Congo proved, but was guilty of flirting with Germany, as shown by his reception of Kaiser Wilhelm II in Ostend. In March 1890, Charles Baudelaire reinforced these deprecatory views with the posthumous publication of notes on his ill-starred stay in Belgium from 1864 to 1866, late in his life. Baudelaire had little good to say of his host country, its people, or its culture.

Against these hostile views we may, however, set the ample evidence that a majority of Parisian critical voices were lifted in praise and support of Maeterlinck's early work in drama and the essay. These voices ranged from conservative academics to the many author-critics actively judging the literary output of their peers. Among those leading academic critics having taken the grand mantle of Charles Augustin Sainte-Beuve, both Fernand Brunetière and Gustave Lanson were lukewarm towards Maeterlinck, but Emile Faguet was enthusiastic in his support. An impressive list of admirers among fellow authors began with Adolphe Retté, who in *Art et Critique* (January 1890) beat Mirbeau to the punch by proclaiming in regard to *Princess Maleine*: 'Henceforth, the proof is made; there is a symbolist theatre.' Unfortunately for Retté his review was ignored, and it fell to Mirbeau to

set the ball rolling later that year. Mallarmé – amazingly to us now, he was struggling then to be recognized – added his voice to the growing acclaim. Approving
noises came also from Paul Valéry, Henri de Régnier, and Romain Rolland. Jules
Lemaître and Anatole France both resisted the lure of Symbolism but appreciated
Maeterlinck. Lemaître went as far as to call Maeterlinck the 'poet of the unconscious', thereby proposing him indirectly as a forerunner of the psychologizing
of Marcel Proust, André Gide, and the surrealists. Rémy de Gourmont, sceptical
but fair, gave an overall thumbs-up to the plays, as well as being probably the first
to perceive a continuity rather than a disjunction between Maeterlinck's plays
and his essays. For his part, Gide wrote to his mother in 1894 that 'at present in
France, we don't have any writer who comes close to Maeterlinck'. Four years later,
when *Wisdom and Destiny* appeared, Gide noted Maeterlinck's changed outlook
and attributed it to an irresistible double attraction, that of life and of Nietzsche,
a combination 'enough to bowl anyone over', though Maeterlinck's thinking was
closer to Henri Bergson's 'creative evolution' than to Nietzsche's iconoclasm – and
was even closer to the transcendental moralism of Ralph Waldo Emerson.

Beyond France and Belgium, Maeterlinck's reputation grew exponentially via
a plethora of translations, often coming close on the heels of the original French
publications and occasionally predating them, and via countless theatrical performances in the United Kingdom, the United States, Austria, Italy, Spain, Greece,
Denmark, Russia, Poland, Romania, Bulgaria, Turkey, and Japan, to name but
several countries in thrall to his work. Indeed, as a growing number of recent
reception studies have shown, there seemed to be no country on the global map
that did not succumb in some measure to a new cult, called by one French critic
'Maeterlinckophilia'.

1901: The buzz of the bee

By the early years of the twentieth century, Maeterlinck was a highly reputed
author in three genres: poetry, drama, and the essay. Within the next decade he
would find himself gaining worldwide renown mainly from the successes of *The
Life of the Bee* and *The Blue Bird*, and from the central role played by Georgette
Leblanc in furthering his career. If we view his celebrity in contemporary terms
– that is, as determined more by visibility and publicity than by artistic accomplishment alone – then both his open cohabitation with Georgette, which
scandalized conservative society, and his bitter dispute with Debussy over casting
her in the operatic version of *Pelleas and Melisande,* added an element of notoriety
to his rapidly growing fame.

Following the successes of *The Treasure of the Humble* and *Wisdom and Destiny*,
Maeterlinck realized he had a winning formula: the treatment of moral and philosophical issues written in a poetic and accessible style. The time was ripe for him
to tackle scientific subjects in personal essay form. He did so in a series of four

outstanding book-length nature essays published during the first three decades of the century. Three were entomological – on the lives of bees, ants, and termites – and one botanical – on the intelligence of flowers – and a rapt and voracious readership devoured them all.

The discourse of these essays bases itself on philosophical and aesthetic responses to methodical nature studies either by Maeterlinck himself, in the case of the first two, or by others. This romantic-scientific approach, already over a century old when Maeterlinck adopted it, fell out of fashion as the dialogue between the sciences and the humanities – despite spirited defences by such luminaries as Albert Einstein, Alfred North Whitehead, and Aldous Huxley – gave way to new specialist and technocratic norms. The appeal of Maeterlinck's amateur insight to such a wide readership until the late 1930s points to the difficult task of communicating scientific knowledge to the general public, and anticipates the critical juncture of the 'Two Cultures' debate opened in Britain in 1959 by C. P. Snow.

The first of the essays, on the bee, remains a perfect example of Maeterlinck's engagement with the 'vulgar' in the best sense of a word which in French carries little of the negative meaning it has in English. For Maeterlinck, the life of the bee permits us to speculate doubly: on the role of instinctive behaviour and on the application of intelligent insight. His essay reflects the optimism he felt at the time; his comparisons between apiarian and human societies are encouraging and reassuring.

Despite his growing confidence as an essayist, we may wonder if he expected his study of bees to become an international bestseller comparable in our day to the mass-market fiction of a John Grisham or a J. K. Rowling. *The Life of the Bee* fitted the bill for an audience eager to redefine its relationship to nature at a time when scientific discovery and technological progress offered much new knowledge, but threatened in their increasing specialization to alienate the average person. Tapping a readership hungry for science made poetic and comprehensible, yet still deemed technically praiseworthy later by eminent entomologists such as William Morton Wheeler and Karl von Frisch, the book took off like a rocket. Published initially in German, its first French edition, by Fasquelle in Paris, sold 237,000 copies, a massive figure by today's standards. Edition followed edition in many languages, and after a wartime lull the work continued to sell steadily until mid-century, to the sum of around half a million copies. As late as 1949, the playwright Thornton Wilder said of its transatlantic impact that 'no work of natural history has gained the success of *The Life of the Bee*: a simplified version of that book has played a major role in the intellectual and scientific development of American children'.

In 1901 also, Maeterlinck's bitter dispute with the notoriously unreliable if equally reticent Debussy only served to place him further in the public eye. The author was not in the least bit musical; he was tone-deaf, in fact. But as Georgette saw an acting opportunity for herself, he weighed in on her behalf. Debussy, though hesitantly, promised her the part of Mélisande, only to change his mind on discovering the greater potential of the Scottish singer Mary Garden in the role. Maeterlinck took legal action against the composer and, it is surmised, even threatened him physically, but all to no avail. The show opened at the Opéra-Comique in a production by Albert Carré on 30 April 1902. Maeterlinck expressed both his hope that the opera would fail and his hatred of his own play. In the event, after an initially bewildered audience response, Debussy's subtle marriage of words to music made the opera a great success, one that was bolstered by the nightly support, outside and inside the theatre, of a devoted set of young enthusiasts – including the future novelist Georges Duhamel – known as the 'Pelleasters', a fan club rather more devoted to Debussy than to Maeterlinck, and one that prefigured the screen subcultures of *Star Trek*, *The Rocky Horror Picture Show*, and *Twilight* today.

At a moment when Maeterlinck's celebrity centred on his essays and on his quarrel with Debussy, a new play, *Monna Vanna*, opened on 17 May 1902, less than three weeks after the opera, in a production by Lugné-Poe at the Théâtre de l'Oeuvre. Georgette exacted a measure of revenge for her snub by Debussy by taking the leading role in a play that Maeterlinck had written expressly with her in mind. And he knew better than simply to offer more of the same evanescent, mysterious, allusive fare that had distinguished his earlier work. *Monna Vanna*, by contrast, is clear, forceful, and energetic. Based on a fifteenth-century Italian story about a strong and beautiful but troubled woman, it was a perfect vehicle for Georgette.

Monna Vanna received mixed reviews, but audiences everywhere loved it. Its commercial success helped to make Maeterlinck a wealthy man, while Georgette milked it for her and her partner's benefit. She took its French version to Germany, England, Italy, Greece, Russia, and the United States. The Maeterlinck–Leblanc project was fully on course. The private author quietly brought out one literary smash hit after another, while the public performer happily took their joint show out on the road. The play went over best in the German-speaking world: a sensational premiere in Berlin in October 1902 was followed by over 400 performances in Germany and Austria. And nothing is new under the sun, since a healthy trade existed in what today we would call 'tie-ins': *Monna Vanna* hats, gloves, and corsets flew off the shelves.

We should not underestimate the part Georgette played in creating Maeterlinck's celebrity. It is often said that opposites attract; Maurice, the shy loner, found a foil in Georgette, the extroverted socialite. His self-styled 'reminiscent' biographer Mahony (1979) suggests that 'without her appetite for vibrant living, Maeterlinck might not have done as well in his career'. The critic Roland Mortier in 1962 was in no doubt: '[she] very rapidly made herself the interpreter, the commentator, the secretary and virtually the impresario of Maeterlinck in France and abroad'.

Not one to rest on his laurels nor to waste precious time on being seen and feted in public, Maeterlinck capped a momentous 1902 by publishing another essay collection, *The Buried Temple*, which kept the optimistic tone of his popular metaphysics. Furthermore, *pace* Freud, it suggested that to accept our subconscious may be the key to a happy, harmonious life insofar as we need to find a balance between illusion and reality, as well as among ideas of past, present, and future. Fairly commonsensical advice, we may agree, and the volume more than satisfied its many readers yet again. At this stage, with Georgette at his side, with critics bedazzled by his elegant thoughtfulness, with an audience waiting on his every word, and with his books selling like hot cakes, Maeterlinck could do no wrong. Within a decade it would get even better for him, but ultimately it would be at the cost both of his relationship with Georgette and of his sunnier outlook on life.

Amid the excitement of *The Life of the Bee*, the spat with Debussy, and the successful dramatic turn of *Monna Vanna*, Maeterlinck continued to write other, if lesser, plays, and other varied essay collections. His preference for a solitary life out of the spotlight boosted his literary productivity. He had become famous almost despite himself and he had Georgette beating his drum, so he saw no reason to question his situation. Nonetheless two plays, *Ariane and Bluebeard* and *Sister Beatrice*, almost got lost in 1901 amid the buzz of the bee. *Joyzelle* followed in 1903 and *The Miracle of St Anthony*, first in German, in 1904. Despite its title and the themes of four of its essays, *The Double Garden* (1904), dedicated to Buysse, was not a major part of his expanding botanical studies but rather a warm and generous appraisal of all living things. The leading piece, published separately in translation, became one of his best loved essays, 'On the death of a small dog'.

Such was the international Maeterlinck fad that his works often appeared sooner abroad than in France. The Germans and the English were the first to publish translations of several of his essays and plays. That it took until 1919 for a French edition of *The Miracle of St Anthony* to appear returns us to the ambiguous nature of Maeterlinck's fame in France. He was the most widely read author in the French language in the early years of the century, yet the French remained reluctant to admit him to their literary pantheon. Though he wrote beautifully and poetically, his name was still not quite right, his mythos was still too Germanic, his 'vulgarity' was still a little suspect in the severe eyes of academics, and his willful detachment from the crowd was no longer admired as an exemplary principle but regretted as an unseemly personal flaw.

From 1903, Maeterlinck and Georgette began to spend their winters in Grasse, in the Maritime Alps, in an area that he described as 'the most wonderful in the world', one that stimulated his interest in flowers and their scents. In 1906, he acquired the Villa des Quatre Chemins in Grasse, leaving Paris for good and finding a haven where he worked for up to ten hours daily on his botanical book and carried out experiments in hybridization. The end product was his second great nature essay, *The Intelligence of Flowers* (1907), acclaimed once more by the critics and the public, its blend of romantic nature philosophy and evolutionary science appealing to conservative and progressive tastes alike. Maeterlinck hewed closer to Lamarck's vitalism and his gentler theory of adaptation than to Darwinism, which was perceived by many intellectuals as a morally inferior scheme. Darwin nonetheless had shared both Maeterlinck's fear for the future of humanity and his agnostic turn, while retaining a hope that belief in God might be reconciled with science by way of an evolutionary theism.

The Intelligence of Flowers belongs to a long tradition of botanical discourse in literature, beginning with the ancients and brought into the modern world by such exponents as Rousseau, Bernardin de St Pierre, Goethe, Ruskin, and Emily Dickinson. Ruskin, for instance, considered botany to be as much a biographical as a descriptive matter. In the preface to *Modern Painters* (1844), he claims 'the difference between the mere botanist's knowledge of plants, and the great poet's or painter's knowledge of them' is that 'the one notes their distinctions for the sake of swelling his herbarium, the other, that he may render them vehicles of expression and emotion'.

In that same year, 1907, the couple rented an old abbey in which they had been interested for a number of years. Their life there would represent the paradox of Maeterlinck's celebrity: his own desire for solitude and silence matched by his, or rather more Georgette's, need to live visibly as figures of public interest. The abbey was a semi-ruined former Benedictine community in St Wandrille, in a quiet corner of the Normandy countryside not far from the city of Rouen. The abbey and its grounds were sprawling. Though he sought a rural retreat where he could both enjoy nature and feed his already highly developed historical imagination, he and Georgette occasionally held court there to the delight of a press that eagerly reported their activities to an enthusiastic readership. Among their house guests were Dame Nellie Melba, Konstantin Stanislavsky, and Verhaeren. The highlight of their activities was a series of theatrical performances, with attendance by strict invitation only, which the couple mounted in August 1909 and 1910 using different parts of the abbey and its demesne as stage or backdrop. These performances, which they called *Fêtes Bleues*, were mainly of Maeterlinck's own plays, including *Pelleas and Melisande,* but on 28 August 1909 they presented his own translation of *Macbeth*, with Georgette in full character as the calculating facilitator at the tragic hero's side.

Their summer home until 1914, when the German advance on France forced them to evacuate, St Wandrille was an exotic location, a mirror image, whether or not he liked it, of Maeterlinck's romantic leanings and artistic imagination. Yet he saw it first and foremost as offering an ideal escape from the madding crowd for a man uneasy at his astronomical rise to fame and fortune, a man who liked nothing more than to follow a daily routine of mental and physical activities. A reserved and high-strung individual endowed nonetheless with virility and athleticism, Maeterlinck viewed his domestic environment as vital to his health, peace of mind, and continuing literary output. He would crave even more breathing space as his fame, considerable as it was by 1907, poised to enter an even greater phase in the course of the next twenty years.

1908: There'll be blue birds (all) over

The seclusion of St Wandrille in the summer of 1908 allowed Maeterlinck to put the finishing touches to what would prove to be his most popular and enduring play, *The Blue Bird*. Based on a Christmas story he had been commissioned to write for *Le Figaro* in 1905, the dream quest of a richly symbolic blue bird by two children was the ultimate expression of his romantic vision, his soon to fade optimism, and his contentment with life. Even so, it has its darker shades. Maeterlinck called it a fairy story, a genre that is never as innocent as it might seem, and the play enters a twilight zone of dislocated time and space. Maeterlinck was a Belgian, after all, and who better than they at conjuring the strange and surreal in language and image?

Yet again, it was Maeterlinck's enthusiasts beyond France who made the play so popular. Stanislavsky put it on stage first in September 1908 at the Art Theatre of Moscow. It hit the boards in New York in 1910 and finally premiered in Paris at the Théâtre Réjane in March 1911. One of the young actresses in that production was the petite and vivacious Renée Dahon, with whom Maeterlinck later fell in love, and whom he married in 1919 following the acrimonious demise of his long-time relationship with Georgette.

The immediate success of the play triggered a 'Blue Bird' craze which was extraordinary even by today's levels of showbiz hype. It has never gone fully out of production in Russia, not even during the bleakest years of Soviet rule. Following its debut in New York, it enjoyed forty-four performances in the first month and a half. Moving from Manhattan to Brooklyn, it was performed over 100 times in two months. It then went to Canada and around the United States, enjoying 600 performances in front of 2 million spectators. In Britain, where Shaw, Henry James, and Max Beerbohm were among the notables attending the 1909 premiere in London, audiences could not get enough of it both on page and on stage: the 1909 translation went through twenty-five editions in two years, while in London performances up to twice daily ran for six months from December 1909.

Even the notoriously hard to please Parisian critics were impressed by the play's enchanting blend of poetry and philosophy, a dramatic equivalent of the formula Maeterlinck was applying so persuasively and lucratively to his essay writing. The blue bird became a widespread symbol of happiness, and the long-term effect of the play's popularity would not have been inconsequential in our own over-heated market for tie-ins to cultural products: songs, picture books, clothing, crockery, jewellery, notepaper, confectionery, playing cards, and ladies' hats were among the related paraphernalia. The silver screen also got in on the act, with two silent versions and a 1940 production with a good script and lavish visuals, but which suffered both from being pushed as a vehicle for Shirley Temple and from a mission impossible of being forced to compete with *The Wizard of Oz*.

We may imagine Maeterlinck's horror as his image appeared everywhere in the press and in framed portraits sold in department stores. Stories abounded of his mysteriousness, while all manner of events in his honour took place mostly in his absence. Quite simply, in the early 1910s, he was the most renowned author in the world. Yet at the height of his fame, Maeterlinck showed his discomfiture by rejecting or resisting various attempts to crown him. In 1910, it was reported that the French Academy was ready to induct him into its ranks, if he would agree to take French citizenship. Doubting the sincerity of this rumour, he made it clear that he was not about to renounce his nationality. Following the outbreak of hostilities in 1914, another attempt led by recently elected president of the republic Raymond Poincaré also came to nothing, though on this occasion not entirely owing to Maeterlinck's refusal, as some academicians had resurrected the 'Germanic rather than French' objection. In the same year, the Academy expressed its wish to hold an event in Maeterlinck's honour, a suggestion he declined, recommending instead that Verhaeren be chosen in his place. His deference to Verhaeren showed itself again in an unsuccessful request that his Nobel Prize be shared by his fellow Belgian. However, this did not prevent Maeterlinck from accepting this greatest of all literary honours in 1911.

The Swedish Academy accorded it to him more for his plays, with their innovative concepts within largely traditional settings, than for his essays, which it viewed as controversial and even provocative in their agnosticism and sceptical view of organized religion. True to form, Maeterlinck – like another reclusive type, Samuel Beckett, fifty-eight years later – declined to attend the prizegiving ceremony in Stockholm, using a bout of influenza as a diplomatic excuse. Nonetheless, he joined members of the Belgian royal family at a tribute to him held at the Théâtre de la Monnaie in Brussels.

Maeterlinck grew sympathetic to the political left, especially as that wing had identified its own aspirations with later passages in *The Intelligence of Flowers*, where the author writes, for instance, of 'our social duty'. His sympathy manifested itself off the page in his moral and financial support of repeated strikes in Belgium from 1902 to 1914. Prompted by Georgette, he had grown aware of the poverty and inequality of large sectors of the working class, and was unable to reconcile this situation with his formerly uplifting view of human life. His political position, however, was inconsistent and reactive rather than committed, but he preferred it that way. Always with one eye on the populist angle, Georgette had encouraged him to think radically and to make gestures of solidarity with the lower orders. Once she was out of the author's life, he settled by the 1920s into a conservative and more complacent existence with Renée.

Those years (1901–14) of unparalleled literary success masked a gradual change in Maeterlinck's hitherto serene view of the world. Apart from his resistance to celebrity, which was due to his temperament and so was nothing new, a number of events quashed his optimism to usher in a lengthy period of pessimism and doubt which made his early Symbolist uncertainties pale by comparison. In 1911, a year in which he swapped his winter home in Grasse for the appropriately named Villa des Abeilles (bees) in Nice, Maeterlinck's mother died, sending him into a neurasthenic state which was mitigated only by the increasing allure of Renée Dahon. Meanwhile, his relationship with Georgette was already showing deep cracks, especially in light of her numerous affairs with other men and women. Exiled to Paris, they stuck together throughout the First World War, but by 1919 Georgette had left for good. Her departure freed Maeterlinck to marry Renée early that year. His investigation of spiritualism and reincarnation in the 1913 essay *Death* led to several of his works being placed summarily on the Catholic Index of banned books. Though this fresh notoriety could hardly have lifted his sagging spirits, he responded with indifference – 'What importance? Rome is a long way away' – and anyway the book sold well. An expanded version of the essay appeared in 1919 under the title *Our Eternity.*

The German invasion of Belgium in 1914 came as a shock to Maeterlinck, who only eleven years earlier had extolled Germany as the 'moral conscience of the world', but now felt duty bound to condemn her criminality and adopt a 'necessary hatred' of that nation. He had enjoyed some of his greatest successes in Germany and Austria, where audiences had proved understandably receptive to his Germanic sensibility. At first he volunteered for active service, but he was told that at 52 his greater contribution would be to use his celebrity to write and speak internationally on behalf of his native land. This he willingly agreed to do by writing pamphlets and speaking out, notably in neutral Italy where crowds swarmed around his hotel and waited on his every word. A poor orator, he found his new role taxing, though he also travelled in that capacity to Spain and England. That he still enjoyed an awkward relationship with the Belgian establishment only served to make his task more difficult. Unsurprisingly, given the context of its creation, his patriotic play *The Mayor of Stilemonde* (1917), with its contemporary and programmatic narrative, was an anomaly within his dramatic oeuvre. Maeterlinck was doing the right thing by his country, but the entire war situation was proving unconducive to both his literary life and his peace of mind.

At the cessation of hostilities in 1918, Maeterlinck was nominated as a founding member of the Belgian Royal Academy of Language and Literature, and was named a count and a grand officer of the Order of Leopold by King Albert the First. Though he eventually accepted the royally appointed title of count in 1932, at the earlier juncture he had refused to take the titles, which seemed insignificant to him in the wake of a terrible war that left him more doubtful than ever of the goodness and wisdom of humankind. His celebrity was about to make one last extraordinary surge, but behind the sustained public image lay now a wearied and disillusioned man.

1919: First he takes Manhattan

In postwar Europe, Maeterlinck's star shone less brightly than before. He was no longer as widely admired by critics, while his own literary output, though remaining steady, lacked the spark of his prewar work. Yet his books continued to sell both in their original editions and in many translations, which followed one another with a degree of frequency of which any other author might only have dreamed. Moreover, his prestige as an international man of letters remained high.

If his light was dimming on his own continent, then the opposite held true across the pond, where his first trip to the United States – on a lecture tour in the grand tradition of Dickens, Thackeray, Wilkie Collins, and Wilde – set off another craze for him and his work. The acclaim he received compared not only to the *Blue Bird* years but later to the mobbing of Charlie Chaplin and other film stars, and much later to the arrival of the Beatles in New York in 1964.

Quietly working in his garden and on his books, still in the honeymoon of his marriage, Maeterlinck was initially unenthusiastic about attending the premiere of Albert Wolff's adaptation of *The Blue Bird* at New York's Metropolitan Opera. Beside his dislike of public appearances, like many European intellectuals of his time he had serious misgivings about the worth of American society and culture. However, following in Georgette's footsteps, Renée encouraged him to accept the invitation, as did his publisher, especially since the promise of a lecture tour added variety and promotional spice to the trip. Though he cared little for such things, the prospect was of another potential gold mine of book sales.

Amid widespread coverage in the press and in silent newsreels, Maeterlinck and his young bride arrived in New York on the SS *Paris* on Christmas Eve, 1919. Welcoming banners and large crowds greeted their disembarkation and procession into Manhattan. This hullabaloo was due as much to his war work as to his literary renown, and also to the similarly feted arrival three months earlier of his monarch, King Albert I. Besieged in his hotel, Maeterlinck was unable to emerge without being importuned like a film star. To his consternation, Manhattan went crazy for a week over the '*Blue Bird* campaign' cannily planned and executed by the Met. It culminated in the opera premiere on the evening of 27 December. At the final curtain Maeterlinck reluctantly took several bows. The inevitable razzamatazz was far from matching his self-image of a private, restrained European man of letters, and with the best will in the world he found the pervading mercenary values superficial and distasteful.

He must also have shuddered inwardly at the prospect of lecturing, given his retiring personality and his awkwardness as a public speaker. Mahony recounts how, for his major speech at Carnegie Hall, Maeterlinck chose the theme of the soul's immortality. He was asked to deliver it in English from a phonetic script which would compensate for his poor command of the spoken language. His tutor for the lecture, Sheridan Russell (son of Maeterlinck's impresario Henry Russell), made little headway with the speaker, whose thin voice exacerbated his linguistic deficiencies. Russell reportedly said, 'You might as well get me to try to lift an elephant as to try to teach him English.' In the event, Maeterlinck made a recondite speech which went over the heads of most of his listeners. At one point he switched to his native language after an embarrassing delay in which Sheridan Russell retrieved the French text from Maeterlinck's hotel room. Despite this inauspicious start to his tour, which was summarily cancelled to his great relief, Maeterlinck's popularity knew no bounds. The New York socialites lionized him at their events, while the masses stopped him in the streets. True to his reticent nature, he shrank from the constant demand for his company on the part of patricians and plebeians alike.

His American odyssey took one further turn when Samuel Goldwyn invited him to Hollywood to join his first group of 'Eminent Authors' and to work freely on adaptations of his own material in the form of stories with potential for filming, as these were still the days of silent cinema. Goldwyn was not the only movie mogul to boost his cultural capital in this manner; for instance, Jesse Lasky brought over Somerset Maugham, and much later Louis B. Mayer imported Evelyn Waugh. Many prominent American authors – William Faulkner, F. Scott Fitzgerald, and Raymond Chandler among the best known – were also invited to board this train, with wildly varying degrees of success. On paper, such artistic marriages seemed heaven-made, but more often than not they proved to be closer to hell. In the case of Maeterlinck, Goldwyn saw it more as an opportunity to elevate his cultural status in Hollywood by trading on the author's prestige than as an expectation that his initiative would bear much saleable fruit. Goldwyn laid on a private railroad car for the cross-country journey, one that in classic American barnstorming style included multiple stops for flesh-pressing and photo opportunities. What must have struck Maeterlinck as an exercise in poor taste was offset by his respect for the ingenuousness of the average citizens he met along the line, and by his admiration of the magnificent natural surroundings. The beauty of the Pacific coast, especially at Santa Monica, where he and Renée stayed, reminded him of the Côte d'Azur and helped in one respect to make him feel somewhat at home in California.

Maeterlinck's three-month place in the sun courtesy of Goldwyn yielded little other than a $100,000 cheque for his trouble. That he flabbergasted the producer by submitting a script about a bee is apocryphal, but consistent with an alliance that was mismatched from the start. The two scripts he completed – 'The power of the dead' and a fairy tale, 'Blue feathers' – failed to pass muster as potential screen vehicles, though in 1945 Maeterlinck sued unsuccessfully for plagiarism of 'The power of the dead' in a celebrated *film noir*, Fritz Lang's *The Woman in the Window*. In his 1983 play *Tales from Hollywood*, Christopher Hampton skewers the absurdity of such author–studio arrangements. In one scene, a reincarnated Ödön von Horvath, the Hungarian-born German author who died in 1938, suggests to an incredulous mogul, Art Nicely, that his sequel to *Bedtime for Bonzo* would have the hero – presumably Ronald Reagan again – falling in love with the chimpanzee.

By May 1920, Maeterlinck and Renée were ready to go home. They sailed from New York to Le Havre and thence to Nice. Completely exhausted by his trip, Maeterlinck entered a welcome phase of withdrawal behind the doors of his villa, where he returned to his writing and enjoyed the serenity of his surroundings. Though the 1920s yielded many pleasures – he and Renée travelled widely and fairly privately for a change – more troubles brought with them more nervous instability. The couple lost a child. Then the appearance of Georgette's *Souvenirs* reopened old wounds; among other unflattering observations, she claimed that she deserved the credit for his success and that he had stolen many of her own creative ideas. Though her account tasted of sour grapes, her accusations stung Maeterlinck, a sensitive soul at the best of times. Wisely, he kept his reactions mainly to himself.

St Wandrille having been returned after the war to the Benedictines according to the original lease agreement, Maeterlinck cast around for a new summer home, and in 1924 found the fifteenth-century Château de Médan, also on the Seine, though closer to Paris. The sixteenth-century poet Pierre de Ronsard had stayed there, and more recently it had been the subject of several canvases by Paul Cézanne. And though Maeterlinck was attached to the Villa des Abeilles, he could not resist the opportunity in 1930 to purchase at a knockdown price a larger, more luxurious home in Nice, the Château de Castellamare, which overlooked the sea. With a heartfelt touch he rechristened it the Villa d'Orlamonde ('Out of the world'), taking the name from the seventh of the *Twelve Songs*, his verse collection from 1896. Life at Orlamonde represented his deep-seated urge to detach himself even further from public view. Admitting only closest friends to the house and refusing all interviews with journalists, he became a virtual recluse.

Still esteemed by most critics, if far less avidly, Maeterlinck continued to write plays and essay collections throughout the 1920s and 1930s. With his fame secured he had little left to prove to a faithful readership, but much of his writing now lacked the originality and verve of his earlier work. Increasingly stoical in tone and resembling the thought experiments practiced by analytical philosophers and theoretical scientists, his writing revisited our approach to the mysteries of life and death via a range of spiritual and psychic experiences. His occultism, particularly in *The Great Secret* (1921), was not to everyone's taste: rationalists and Christians alike attacked it. There were fewer high points in his output, though *The Life of Space* (1928) rapidly sold 50,000 copies. Its astrophysical prescience caught the attention of Einstein as well as that of a general audience excited by the relativity of time and space. Surrealist icons like Gustave Apollinaire and André Breton admired his poetry (especially *Hothouses*), but Maeterlinck, now the philosopher and poetic scientist, dismissed that portion of his work as insignificant. To great acclaim, two more nature essays completed the set of four begun by those on the bee and the flower. *The Life of Termites* (1926) sold 80,000 copies in two years plus another 40,000 over the next decade, while *The Life of Ants* (1930) enjoyed a print run of 70,000, an equally impressive number for a book of that kind at the time.

These two essays showed Maeterlinck's growing despair of the human condition. The termite world is 'a republic of the night', one we may admire for its brilliant design and utter efficiency while recoiling from its unceasing misery. It is a world in which winged, sighted workers obediently and impotently serve a perfectly organized and extremely durable community run by huge, blind, earthbound guards and presided over by a monarchy that is totally dependent for survival on the goodwill of its lowest subjects. Again, Maeterlinck invites us to compare this world with that of our own, and the picture he draws is not a pretty one.

He is more praising of the indefatigable ant, whose intelligence he finds superior to, though less poetic than, that even of the bee. However, he sees no ultimate merit in the ants' many qualities, since their lives appear futile and without reward, despite the unselfishness of their 'social' pouch, an appendage that carries food they regurgitate ecstatically to share with others. He contrasts their altruism and self-sacrifice to human egotism. Indeed, any evidence of altruism in the natural world remains a problem for evolutionary science, though a compromise perhaps lies in the theory of ecological symbiosis rather than that of gene-centered natural selection. Seemingly hungry for further insights into insect life, Maeterlinck's audience took to *The Glass Spider* (1932), but many readers were surprised to discover that the book not only dealt with a strange aquatic insect also known as a water- (or diving-bell) spider but also included essays on pigeons.

Nothing in Maeterlinck's later plays could match the startling innovation and sheer brio of his achievements up to and including *The Blue Bird*. His only comedy, *The Miracle of St Anthony* (1919), is noteworthy chiefly for the absence of those earlier qualities, while the strange play *Princess Isabelle* (1935), set in the Flemish town of Geel, still known today as a haven for the insane, served mainly as a vehicle for Renée's thespian talent. One play for which the Germans never forgave Maeterlinck was *The Mayor of Stilemonde*, and as war clouds gathered again in 1939, he was warned that his name might be on a Gestapo black list. He and Renée stayed in France as long as they felt safe, but eventually had to leave for Portugal and the protection of his friend, the prime minister (and later dictator) Antonio Salazar. But even Portugal proved to be a risky location as fears grew of a Nazi invasion backed by fascist Spain. Once again more out of necessity than enthusiasm, Maeterlinck and his wife set out in 1940 for the shores of the United States.

In a year that saw the death of Georgette Leblanc, the Maeterlincks arrived in New York on 12 July. Despite the relative absence of fervour awaiting their re-entry, Maeterlinck was still harangued by reporters and received lucrative invitations to write articles for the press, many of which he accepted simply as a means of financing their unintended stay in the country. And with showbiz entrepreneurs still alive to the potential of Maeterlinck's works, it looked for a while as if he might recapture the public's attention. But times had changed along with audience tastes, so there was no return to the feverish days of *The Blue Bird*. At least *Pelleas and Melisande* returned to the operatic repertoire. Forgetting his resentment of Debussy, Maeterlinck consented to attend a performance in Philadelphia in 1941. He celebrated his 80th birthday in 1942, saw out the rest of the Second World War stateside, and carried on writing, if by then at a slow pace and without comment on the resurgence of German aggression. He wrote mainly as a participant in the rat race of American journalism, to enter which he had been disinclined but obliged, and which showed little appetite anyway for his profound and measured reflections.

Something of a fixture in New York, Maeterlinck remained a popular figure, but his health started to fail. After the war, he and Renée decided to escape the bitter northern winter by renting an apartment in Palm Beach, Florida, in 1946. But this salubrious change came too late. In 1947 he developed bronchial pneumonia, and perhaps sensing an ending he decided to return to France, arriving by ocean liner in Marseilles in August. Orlamonde needed much repair after the ravages of German occupation. In 1948 he published *Blue Bubbles,* a valedictory work, its subtitle 'Happy Memories' introducing an engaging set of fragmentary texts full of allusion and reminiscence. He died at Orlamonde on 6 May 1949, in the same year as his compatriot, the Expressionist painter James Ensor, and in a year when the Nobel Prize was awarded to Faulkner, a citizen of his adopted land of wartime exile.

More than fifteen minutes of fame

Though widely reported, news of Maeterlinck's death failed to create the stir associated with the events in his life up to the 1920s. It would have been extraordinary had he been able to maintain the level of international celebrity he had enjoyed for two decades following the worldwide success of *The Life of the Bee*. Though French publishers largely lost interest in Maeterlinck's work in the immediate postwar period, it continued to appear abroad. In 1962, the centenary of Maeterlinck's birth, the linguist (and early proponent of francophone Belgian literature) Joseph Hanse remained optimistic about the state of the author's reputation, given the 'worldwide interest' in the anniversary and the number of studies devoted to his work. Over a thirty-year period after Maeterlinck's death, his books reappeared and his plays were still performed, albeit rather less frequently and prominently. This relative decline in interest merely furthered a process that had already begun in the last twenty years of his life, when his essay collections had made less impact and he had entered a phase of semi-retirement.

Influenced by new approaches to literary criticism and to theatrical methods in the 1960s and 1970s, the 1980s ushered in a period in which Maeterlinck's work has been subjected to an ongoing reconsideration, while his erstwhile fame as an author and public figure has benefited from the rise of celebrity studies within academia. In recent years, critical reassessments and new translations of Maeterlinck have appeared from scholars such as Paul Gorceix and Arnaud Rykner in France, Patrick McGuinness in Great Britain, and David Willinger and Daniel Gerould in the United States. Yet in 2000, the blurb for the proceedings of a colloquium in France on Maeterlinck could say 'still quoted, rarely discussed, Maeterlinck is at once very present in our culture and strangely absent from the dominant strain of criticism'. And in the *Times Literary Supplement* (6 January 2012), a columnist describes 1862, the year of Maeterlinck's birth, as a 'dull' one for sesquicentenaries, which prompted a correspondent to make an excellent 1862 case for Edith Wharton, while rather too eagerly dismissing the 'increasingly obscure' Maeterlinck. Clearly, there is still some way to go in reintroducing his work to a broader audience.

Despite his leading role in European literature during the first half of the twentieth century, Maeterlinck was in many respects a man already out of his time, which may help to explain his lifelong distaste for publicity and fame. Though he was keenly interested in scientific and technological progress and certainly unopposed to it in principle, his defining world view and his literary style were both rooted in Romanticism. It was only in the formal daring of his Symbolist plays that he could claim to be a pioneer of a modernist experimentalism which by the 1930s saw a new generation of ideologically motivated authors leaving him further behind.

A brief moment of posthumous notoriety occurred in 2001 on the appearance in Dutch of *The Curse*, a piece of literary nonfiction by Flemish historian David Van Reybrouck. In this book, his first, the author opened a can of worms by asserting that Maeterlinck, in *The Life of the Termite*, had plagiarized a 1925 study in Afrikaans, *The Soul of the Termite*, by South African scientist Eugène Marais (published in book form in 1934). Marais had claimed that Maeterlinck took among other things from his work the idea of the organic unity of the termitary. Short of funds and addicted to morphine, Marais unsuccessfully sued Maeterlinck before shooting himself dead in 1936. He was thus denied the small consolation of an English translation of his work having resulted from the scandal. Was the episode a storm in a teacup? Maeterlinck clearly failed to give credit to a likely source, but within the conventions of the essay form as he understood it, he felt unconstrained by scholarly expectations of full and precise documentation. Even so, the termite and ant essays, unlike those on the bee and the flower, were based solely on scholarly material and not on personal observations. On the termite, he offered a two-page summary of research on the subject in the course of his introduction, made frequent reference to the studies of others throughout his main text, and appended a bibliography, but nowhere was any mention of Marais's work to be found.

Whatever scholars and critics may deem to be Maeterlinck's place today in a literary canon that has been so thoroughly challenged, even fragmented and inverted, his celebrity remains a remarkable phenomenon. I would argue that it places him fairly alongside Byron, Hugo, Twain, Dickens, and Fitzgerald among few other Western authors in the last 200 years to have held their audience's rapt attention as much for their public image as for the substantial, imaginative, and eloquent language they committed to the page.

2

Out of Denmark: Karen Blixen

Several months of 1972 spent in the sylvan surroundings of the Peace Research College (or hippie commune, if you prefer) at the nineteenth-century Hesbjerg Castle in the Funen countryside west of Odense gave me an appreciation of what life may once have been like on a classic *herregaard* (country estate) of the kind on which Karen Blixen spent much of her life. (The postscript to this essay offers a further glimpse of life at Hesbjerg.) Though I believe I would have liked Blixen's work regardless of her background, my brief experience of that rural environment helped me in a certain way to understand better a person whose life and art were largely defined by the values of the traditional Danish landowning class and by the rarefied atmosphere of its homes.

From an early age Karen Blixen sensed that she was an extraordinary individual, a person who could willingly become a *celebrity* but not a celebrity *author*. Though she went on to become the latter anyway, she saw herself as participating more fully in a grand tradition of oral storytelling. Literary celebrity was an unexpected, if not wholly unwelcome, consequence of drastic changes in the circumstances of her adult life. Even then, in her mind there was always a vulgar element of such fame. In choosing to earn her living from authorship, she made a virtue out of necessity, and in the process discovered – perhaps to her surprise – that her gift of storytelling also presented itself eloquently and effortlessly on the printed page. Her avid readership was in no doubt about it.

Born in 1885, Karen Dinesen came from a marriage between the landed gentry (Dinesen) and the haute bourgeoisie (her mother was a Westenholz, from a family of wealthy merchants). Aged 10, she lost her father Wilhelm, and never ceased to adore his memory or wish herself to become everything she had perceived him to be – noble, brave, and adventurous, an admirable representative of an old and fading way of life. Stricken with syphilis, he killed himself, and ironically his daughter shared in his death too, as many years later she suffered from the same disease contracted from her husband. As a girl, she rebelled against a restricted family life as represented by the pious, cautious, serious, civic-minded values that had made the Westenholzes rich and respectable. In this sense, we may see a parallel with the youth of Virginia Haggard (Chapter 9); like her, but a generation earlier and more offhandedly, Karen studied art in the Paris studios before the Great War of 1914–18.

Following a three-year solitary sojourn among Native Americans in a mid-Western wilderness of the United States, Wilhelm Dinesen had published

Karen Blixen, Copenhagen Airport, 1957

a book in 1889 under the Native American pseudonym of Boganis. Following in her father's footsteps, young Karen Dinesen showed a nascent literary talent too. She published several short stories in Danish magazines, also under a Native American pseudonym, Osceola, but soon thereafter her life took a very different turn. Her fantasy of leading an aristocratic existence materialized in an unexpected marriage to her Swedish cousin, Bror von Blixen-Feineke, with whom she upped sticks and moved to British East Africa to help him run a coffee plantation and eventually take it over on her own.

In the rarefied air, literally and figuratively, of this colonial community, Karen Blixen became a social celebrity. She mixed with a small and peculiar crowd of predominantly British expatriates including nobles, gentlemen, millionaires, politicians, farmers, and soldiers. She knew royalty too: Prince Wilhelm of Sweden proposed her marriage toast (aboard a train from Mombasa to Nairobi), and the Prince of Wales took tea on her farm. But her celebrity came from more than rubbing shoulders with the upper classes. She gained special recognition within this community as a skillful and resourceful entrepreneur, as a female boss on particularly good terms with her native retinue, and when the day's work was done, as a peerless conversationalist and teller of tales.

Within the hothouse of this white minority faction, she gravitated toward those individuals who, like herself, had felt a desire, even a need, to escape from their stultifying native societies in search of a relatively unrestricted way of life. They were rich and privileged, of course, and so had the luxury of living out their dreams. Above all, she was drawn to their inquisitive, freewheeling attitude. She discovered this quality at its most developed in several young British men, such as Berkeley Cole and especially Denys Finch-Hatton, who became her greatest love and whose death in an air accident, along with the failures of both her farm and her marriage to Bror, were the turning-points in her life, events that caused and hastened her reluctant decision to leave Africa and return, distressed in mind and body, to Denmark.

Selling her farm on the outskirts of Nairobi to a property developer, who named his new suburb 'Karen' after her, she left behind her a reputation for having unusually and often eccentrically secured her place in a generally conservative and male-dominated group. On her return to Europe, however, Baroness von Blixen-Feinecke found herself virtually ignored beyond those high social circles in Kenya and Denmark that had confirmed her place in the aristocratic order.

Karen Blixen thus decided to try to publish a collection of stories on which she had worked intermittently for several years. Being unknown as a writer made this already difficult task more so, as her subject matter and style were thoroughly out of step with the evolving nature of Danish literature in the 1930s. To improve her chances of publication, she chose to write in English and under the male semi-pseudonym of Isak ('the one who laughs') Dinesen. One year after completing her manuscript, *Seven Gothic Tales* was published in the United Kingdom and the United States. At the age of 49, she found herself shot into literary stardom by the enormous success of the book. She translated the book herself, and it was published in Denmark as *Syv fantastiske fortællinger* in 1935, but met with a muted critical reception.

Though she was soon uncovered as the author, she maintained that using a pseudonym gave her more freedom to keep a distance between herself and her authorial identity. 'The Baroness' was a fundamental part of a self-image distinct from that of 'Isak Dinesen', the writer. This distinction may also have been partly one of 'Isak's' jokes, a playful 'jesture' that served to remind her followers that she remained at heart in a class of her own, a true amateur of the narrational art.

In the course of her literary career, Karen Blixen often bemoaned her problematic relation to the canon of Danish literature and to its dominant twentieth-century directions. One of those problems is that she was to all extent and purposes as much an English-language author as she was a Danish one. The critic Poul Borum, reflecting on Danish literature in 1979, perceived an umbilical cord tying her to the 'Danish Burns', the Romantic poet and short story writer Steen Steensen Blicher. He also connected Blixen to the later nineteenth-century novelist Meïr Aron Goldschmidt, though the connection seems to be only in Goldschmidt's move to England and his translations of his own work into the English language.

Whatever misgivings Karen Blixen may have had about her sudden literary celebrity, it grew rapidly on the international success of *Out of Africa* (1937, which she translated as *The African Farm*), her memoir of life on her coffee plantation in Kenya. With it, she won over the Danish sceptics who had suspected her initial success to be a fluke, no more than a briefly sensational set of weird and exotic tales. Captivating from the first page, *Out of Africa* is a model page-turner though not of a novelistic kind. Indeed, the mechanics of fiction are conspicuously absent. Written in simple yet elegant prose, it seems to spring from an earlier and more heroic age, one to which the author felt more akin than to an early twentieth-century white-settler society to which she belonged fully yet scorned as stuffy and small-minded. This anachronistic sense helps to explain the generical uncertainty of the memoir. It is what Robert Langbaum calls an 'authentic pastoral', in which the author is neither autobiographer nor diarist but the consummate narrator of a vivid and transcendent world, fully engaged with her subject yet serenely detached from the action. As a result, neither a confessional tone, nor melodramatic and sentimental elements, nor documentary detail weigh it down. Nonetheless she employs a liberal dose of poetic licence as well as avoiding markedly more troubling questions of gender, race, and class.

Let me strike here a cautionary note. Blixen's personal and literary charisma is strong and alluring. We should understand that it was easy for her to idealize her story, and is tempting for us to romanticize it. *Out of Africa* appears as the account of a largely charmed and charming life shared with loyal native retainers and dashingly handsome fellow adventurers, all taking place amid majestic natural surroundings. The glossy 1985 Hollywood film version, starring Meryl Streep as Blixen and Robert Redford as Finch-Hatton, only serves to reinforce this image. We should remember, however, that a driving force in the construction of Blixen's celebrity was her own narcissism, a trait deep-rooted in an archaic and illusory self-image, that of an enlightened and unfettered European aristocrat of an earlier century. In *White Women Writers and Their African Invention*, his 2003 study of Blixen and Olive Schreiner, Simon Lewis reminds us that Blixen was writing *Out of Africa* in the late 1930s about her experience there from 1914 to 1931. We may then realize that her vision in the book is necessarily an elegiac one, born of a 'desire to transform a real past into an ideal picture', and that it generates a 'nostalgic representation of an Edenic Africa, with its silence on the violence of imperialism'. In that sense *Out of Africa*, like its author, is marvellously out of time.

Blixen's mid-life literary renown permitted her to recover a lost social place among the rich and famous at home in Denmark and abroad. For the rest of her life, in between bouts of illness and depression and sometimes even during them, she glittered in the great European cities, notably Paris, London, and Rome. Among those who came to see her or with whom she had audiences were Queen Alexandrine of Denmark, Pope Pius XII, Niels Bohr, John Gielgud, Aldous Huxley, and Timothy Leary. Her celebrity occasionally compromised her, as on her journalistic assignment to Germany at the beginning of the Second World War, when Denmark was still neutral and when the Third Reich, knowing of her command of English and her access to an anglophone readership, attempted to exploit her presence.

The German trip is but one illustration of the many ambiguities and contradictions that tell the story of Karen Blixen's celebrity. She claimed to be on the side of the common people, and her respect for, compassion towards, and loyalty to her African dependants certainly suggests as much. And yet she defined herself against the lower classes. In her African days, as Judith Thurman points out in her 1982 biography, 'her own situation, as one of the greatest feudal overlords in the country, was a paradox, as was the fact that her own *noblesse oblige* in the role gave her such pleasure'. To the manor she was born; on the manor she stayed; only that by the mid-1930s her 'domain' also embraced an international readership eagerly hanging on her every word.

Her first stories composed back in the 1910s had a gothic tinge that came into its own in the seven tales and in her mystery novel *The Angelic Avengers* (*Gengældelsens veje*, 1946), which she wrote under the pseudonym of Pierre Andrézel and claimed had been translated by her secretary Clara Svendsen. She was much more than an author of the gothic, of course, but this side of her talent links her with another modern mistress of the genre, Daphne du Maurier, whose reputation has enjoyed a large and deserved revival in recent years. Both women were neo-Romantics in thrall to storytelling, legend, folklore, and the fast-disappearing ascendancy of the landed gentry and upper classes. As celebrities, however, they were complete opposites. Karen Blixen enjoyed the limelight, if reluctantly as a best-selling author; du Maurier, born into a social whirl centred on London journalism and the theatre thanks to her grandfather George and father Gerald respectively, shrank from public view to seek refuge with her husband 'Boy' Browning in a quiet life as a landed lady on the Cornwall coast.

As Blixen's life refashioned itself around her native land and the fate of its people under occupation by Nazi Germany, so she recovered her national identity and reverted to writing in Danish, with translation into English by her own hand. *The Angelic Avengers* is a minor example, but it is *Winter's Tales* (*Vintereventyr*, 1942)

that proved her continuing popularity despite the methodical change in authorship. In any case, her mastery of both languages – in matters of both technical
command and the far more elusive quality of style – created another facet of her
literary celebrity, as a bilingual author to be spoken of in the same breath as Joseph
Conrad and Vladimir Nabokov, sharing with Nabokov especially a refined style as
well as an affection for the old aristocratic way.

Karen Blixen's status as a *grande dame* of Danish literature drew a group of young
authors to her, though their courtship was not always reciprocated. Based close
to her Rungstedlund home north of Copenhagen, the 'Vedbæk Parnassus' that
coalesced around the journal *Heretica* was particularly solicitous of her opinion
and accord. She developed a notorious relationship with one of these young Turks,
Thorkild Bjørnvig, who chronicled their tempestuous four-year friendship in *The
Pact* (1974), a memoir with the narrative drive of a perfectly turned novel. Eventually they turned on one another, while she dismissed his fellow travellers partly
for their reformulation, under the rising influence of one of their peers, Martin A.
Hansen, of a Christian idealism as first expressed by the Romantic poet N. F. S.
Grundtvig. Their ethical and theological schemata came inevitably into conflict
with her grander metaphysical and pre-bourgeois vision, one that deplored the
fact that since the nineteenth century the Danish people had been, in the words
of G. B. Shaw's lovable rogue Eliza Doolittle in *Pygmalion*, progressively 'delivered
into the hands of middle-class morality', a sanctimonious and constricting
creed that Blixen recalled so painfully from the Westenholz side of her family
experience.

The United States is the country that had first acclaimed her writing and
where she enjoyed an unreserved reputation both for it and for her celebrity role.
Though seriously ill and presenting herself as little more than skin and bones,
she finally realized an ambition by making it across the Atlantic in early 1959.
Her endurance of a hectic round of cultural and social engagements remains an
extraordinary feat, all the more so for her having been in no fit physical state to
have undertaken the trip at all.

We may care little for some of her personality traits and her elitist attitude; her
sheer pluck and determination to live to the fullest cannot be gainsaid. For her,
it was a matter of living up to a personal code of courage, dignity, and honour.
Utilizing a battery of exotic cosmetics and flamboyant clothing, she gamely
concealed her wretched condition with the careless aplomb of a true noble. Photographed at every turn, she delighted in being what today we call a media celebrity.
One of the best-known shots of her American trip is of her holding forth at a New
York luncheon in the company of Carson McCullers, Arthur Miller, and Marilyn
Monroe.

Though she belonged to an age preceding that of the television personality, she
became a media celebrity through her Danish radio talks, which she had begun in
1945. The talks, which she treated rather like royal addresses – or perhaps more so,

presidential addresses in the style of Franklin D. Roosevelt's radio 'fireside chats' with the American people in the 1930s and 1940s – throw an interesting sidelight on her view of that medium and on her relationship to her audience. She referred to her talks as 'meetings' with her listeners, as if these were face-to-face encounters, thus lending a more personal note to the experience. A striking instance of this approach is her 1958 address 'Rungstedlund' in which she described her home, its history, and its natural surroundings as if welcoming the public in person to her estate and giving them a guided tour. She also asked her listeners each to send one *krone* (plus 32 *øre* in postage) in aid of a fund for the future upkeep of her property. And she was also keen to count the numbers so as to gauge the extent of her following. In the event, 8,000 Danes responded to what she called, with wit and characteristic self-esteem, 'the best job of begging I ever heard'.

Gratified by this fulsome response, which extended to her being constantly stopped in the street, she set the greatest store by being recognized not so much for *what* she was, namely the successful author Isak Dinesen, but for *who* she was, namely Baroness Blixen. Though she occasionally appeared on television, the medium of radio appealed more to the storyteller in her, as in performance it was solely to do with the sound of the language and her masterful delivery of it. We sense that she was less enthusiastic about the blunt and distracting visibility of television. Radio suited her aura; one communicated, as she put it, by a 'voice in the ether'.

Hannah Arendt, in her unflattering review of Parmenia Migel's 1967 biography, maintained that Blixen felt it unbecoming to be a professional author, which she had become only after abandoning Africa and losing the love of her life. Her literary renown often embarrassed her, as when the inferior (by her standard) *Angelic Avengers* sold 90,000 copies. For someone who so eagerly took centre stage in social interactions, she avoided the domestic publicity for *Last Tales* (*Sidste fortællinger*, 1957) by going to Rome. She feared, perhaps with reason, that this somewhat contrived and protracted volume did not match her earlier collections despite it selling extremely well internationally, as did too the brilliant collection *Anecdotes of Destiny* (*Skæbne-anekdoter*, 1958) and the less accomplished *Shadows in the Grass* (*Skygger på græsset*, 1960), an afterword to her African story. She had begun to write out of necessity and continued on occasion to do so, even reluctantly assaying the lucrative American magazine market with material that nonetheless included stories of the highest quality, such as 'Babette's feast'.

In 'Rungstedlund' she told her audience that contrary to their expectation of her means, her literary career offered her no more than an erratic and limited income – untenable for someone who hated limits of any kind – and that she felt sorely tried by the tax burden placed on her as a result of her success. She said further that she found working with paper and ink 'distasteful' and that 'merely to become printed matter' was a seriously *déclassé* condition for one whose dominant self-image was of a noble storyteller with a refined sense of narration. Her only ambition, she told Daniel Gillès in her penultimate year, was 'to invent stories, very beautiful stories'. She also admitted to him that she 'detested' literature; by this I suspect she meant the literary *system* as manifested ordinarily in its commercial and critical aspects. Privately, at least, I also suspect she would have delighted in winning the Nobel Prize, for which she was for several years a serious contender. Yet her characteristically canny attitude to such an accolade is captured perfectly in her remark to Ernest Hemingway – the 1954 laureate, who graciously placed her before himself in his own estimation – that his 'kind words' gave her 'as much heavenly pleasure – even if not as much earthly benefit – as would have done the Nobel Prize itself'.

Sceptics may see in these and other pronouncements a serious case of bad faith; others – some in on the joke, so to speak – may see instead in her performances the skillful and at times arrogant prestidigitation of a verbal magician utterly sure of her act and equally sure of her rightful place in the larger scheme of things. Whether one loves or hates her personality – she veered from snobbish and spiteful to charming and compassionate, sometimes all in one conversation – few would deny the truth that she confided to one of her young disciples, Ole Wivel: 'It takes terrible courage to create.'

Postscript: Returning to Mr Vig

Wednesday, 4 October 1972: I moved into a room in Hesbjerg Castle on the Danish island of Funen. I would stay in this imposing bell-towered mansion (completed in 1881) for the next three months; as a doctoral student in England, I was spending one semester at Odense University. I had lasted only two weeks in my first lodgings in a pleasant old house on Kastanievej in the city of Odense. The inspirational quotes from communist fathers placed above the kitchen sink and beneath the bathroom mirror by my hardline fellow tenants proved too much for my broader – though broadly sympathetic – political view. I found the castle, 12 kilometres away and owned by a Mr Jørgen Laursen Vig, much more to my liking.

Sunday, 3 October 2010: almost thirty-eight years to the day since I had embraced the Funen countryside, I flew into Copenhagen and touched Danish soil again. I had returned for a conference on film and European cultures. Conversing with the organizer, Professor Ib Bondebjerg, on the bus to our conference hotel in the old port of Præstø in southeastern Zealand, I recalled teaching high school English in Jutland from 1970 to 1971 and then residing during the following year at Hesbjerg. On hearing this name, he told me of a 2006 documentary, *The Monastery: Mr Vig and the Nun*, made by Danish director Pernille Rose Grønkjær. On returning to the capital, I wasted no time in purchasing a copy at the Danish Film Institute shop. Back home in the United States a few days later, as familiar scenes unfolded before my eyes, I found myself returning to Mr Vig.

Vig came from a family of Jutland farmers, and only later in life did he discover

Jørgen Laursen Vig, Hesbjerg

that his father's family in the eighteenth century had belonged to a rural Lutheran revivalist movement known as *De Stærke Jyder* (Strong Jutlanders), a generational connection that helps perhaps to explain his own predisposition to follow a devotional life on the land. In 1957, at the age of 39 – already a librarian at Copenhagen University and a Lutheran pastor trained in theology, classical philosophy, and Russian – he bought the 100-acre Hesbjerg estate in order to realize his dream of creating a spiritual community inspired by his youthful experience of Benedictine monasteries in Europe and Africa. Surrounded by farm fields and forests, the estate was a beautiful and tranquil place to live. At first, he experimented with a 'folk' high school (a peculiarly democratic Danish institution open to all) at which he offered resident education in return for daily labour on the land.

By the time I arrived, he had already established Hesbjerg as a Peace Research College. It now doubled as a hippie commune attuned to alternative values of the time: East meeting West in spirit and living organically off the land. Studying full-time, I paid a nominal rent for my ground-level room facing woods to the back, while those willing to fix the house and till the land could live in free of charge. Not all, however, were interested in work of that kind. Some were aspiring young artists and writers, while others included urban acid casualties convalescing in the fresh country air. A generally meditative atmosphere gave way occasionally to loud bursts of rock music from rooms whose dominant aromas were of incense and dope; sceptical locals dubbed the castle 'Hashbjerg'. Indian printed cotton was the soft furnishing fabric of choice, while meat was strictly off-menu. Shortly after arriving, while in the kitchen preparing my spaghetti Bolognese dinner, I looked up: flaring nostrils and censorious eyes surrounded me. That evening's experience turned me into a vegetarian for years to come.

A reclusive and rather intimidating figure, Vig rarely emerged from his quarters, which gave directly onto the entrance hall, and he left much of the daily routine to his motley crew of communards. Nonetheless, as the autumn drew to a close, he grandly announced that he would 'light the fire' the next morning. Some of us duly gathered in the antiquated boiler-room to witness him – resplendent in overalls and a balaclava hat – perform an annual ritual, one captured nicely by Grønkjær in her film. One evening, Vig invited me into his library to discuss a poetry translation I happened to be working on. His passion for the humanities and openness to my stumbling efforts impressed me deeply. I felt privileged to have been granted a rare tutorial by this erudite and private man.

Thursday, 21 December 1972: I threw my bags into my beaten-up Ford saloon and left the castle for the last time, eventually arriving back in England before the New Year rolled around.

Christmas, 2005: almost exactly thirty-three years later, Vig died in India at the age of 87. His last days were spent at a peace research conference in the holy city of Benares. He had kept his enthusiastic commitment to a more peaceful and spiritually cleansed world. By then, Grønkjær had finished shooting the film she had begun six years earlier and was editing 100 hours of accumulated footage, having little imagined at the outset how far she would be drawn into the fascinating world of the castle and its owner. She returned to Hesbjerg in 2006 to shoot an unexpected but fitting closing scene to her award-winning film: Vig's funeral service. It took place in a large room which by then served as a church for the Russian Orthodox monastery, entitled by Vig's will to occupy the castle. In my brief time there, the space had been a common room, and one shot captures the black faux-leather easy chairs still in their place to the rear.

Grønkjær focuses on Vig's efforts in his final years to establish this monastery and on his close but often fraught relationship with Sister Amvrosija, a nun who took up residence in 2001 along with several others from a Russian convent. An eccentric confirmed bachelor suddenly found himself having to coexist with a group of women led by someone as strong-willed as himself. We witness these idealistic protagonists being severely tested as they faced the reality of their own stubbornness, of tangled legalities, and of a crumbling building that at the time of my residence was intact, if gently faded, but now sorely in need of extensive structural repairs.

Following the withdrawal of the Russian Orthodox Church largely owing to castle renovation issues, the now Mother Amvrosija moved elsewhere, while an alternative monastic initiative involving a Ukrainian abbot sadly failed. Returning to its status solely as a Peace Research College, with an ecological village leasing part of the estate in a permanent arrangement, Hesbjerg limps on. Though several cultural events have taken place in recent years along with an annual Pentecost festival, the castle's state of disrepair has resulted in communal activities coming temporarily to a halt. A foundation oversees Hesbjerg, but it faces a critical situation in respect of both the huge task of restoring the castle and a difficult ongoing relationship with the Moscow Patriarchate of the Orthodox Church.

Watching the film revived a small but unforgettable part of my own life that had long been stored away in my memory vaults. More than a localized case study of two equally determined individuals, *The Monastery: Mr Vig and the Nun* explores sensitively and often amusingly our indefatigable quest for spiritual fulfilment and for a perfect place to seek it. Well crafted and affectionate in tone, the film is a fine memorial to a cranky but ever thoughtful and sincere man with a lifelong dream of fusing Buddhism and Christianity in a quiet corner of the kingdom of Denmark. For a precious moment, late in life, his dream more or less came true.

Whitwell Elwin by Henry Weigall, RA, 1876

3

Review from the rectory: Whitwell Elwin

The county of Norfolk, England is noted for a plethora of square and round-towered medieval churches, large and small, many of which are strikingly built of local flintstone. In all, there are more than 650 of them – the highest concentration in the world. All the more bewildering therefore is the sight of pinnacles and a minaret rising above farm fields and clustered trees. But then, nothing is as it should be at St Michael the Archangel, Booton, located about one mile to the east of this tiny village. The church represents a nineteenth-century labour of love by its rector, the Reverend Whitwell Elwin: gentleman, literary scholar, and church builder.

Though weakened by eighteenth- and nineteenth-century social developments in the landowning class, a long tradition existed of literary and intellectual rectory life. It was, says Margaret Watt, writing in 1943 on the history of parsons' wives, largely 'the product of a close connection between the Church and the universities' going back to the Elizabethan cleric Richard Hooker. Nor may we overlook, in relation to Elwin, another Norfolk parson, James Woodforde, whose *Diary* (1758–1802), written at Weston Longville, little more than 5 miles from Booton, reveals a domestic and parochial life as subdued and unpretentious as that of Elwin in the following century.

Quirky Victorian churches and literary clergymen have been in the air in recent years with the publication in 2013 of two books: *The Pinecone*, Jenny Uglow's biography of Sarah Losh, daughter of the manor house, child of the Regency period, architect, and builder of St Mary's, Wreay, near Carlisle, in Cumbria; and *The Wry Romance of the Literary Rectory*, Deborah Alun-Jones's account of eight British writers, some of them clergymen, whose connections with various Anglican places of residence have been particularly engaging.

Placing these studies of architecture and literature together in an ecclesiastical context offers a perfect introduction to the life of Whitwell Elwin. When not carrying out his clerical duties or rebuilding his dilapidated medieval church according to his own idiosyncratic vision, Elwin was a notable man of letters, who – like his cousin Frances whom he married in 1838 – was uninterested in wealth or fame. He chose to intersperse his work in the quiet and plainly furnished rectory (unpainted walls, no curtains or carpets) with regular visits to London as a contributor to and sometime editor of the *Quarterly Review*, a Tory periodical founded in 1809 by the firm of John Murray, largely to counter the Whiggish position of its slightly older rival, the *Edinburgh Review*. The historian Asa Briggs describes these two reviews as 'the two great organs of traditional English politics'. Such was Elwin's involvement in the former that in 1853 the Post Office installed a branch at Booton expressly to handle the volume of his mail. In short spurts of energetic activity, he participated fully in the capital's literary life and consorted with many of the leading artistic and intellectual figures of his time. And the same area produced a rival editor: Henry Reeve, who had spent his early years in the city of Norwich, the county seat, and attended its grammar school (my own alma mater), edited the *Edinburgh Review* from 1855 until his death in 1895.

The Elwins were lords of the manor of Booton, a village adjacent to the handsome small market town of Reepham and about 10 miles north-west of Norwich. Long established in Norfolk, the Elwins had bought the estate from the Layer family in 1713, and by the mid-nineteenth century, when Whitwell's elder brother Hastings was squire, they owned over 1,000 acres of land there. The third son of Marsham Elwin, a country gentleman from the village of Thurning a few miles from Booton, Whitwell was born in 1816 and studied at Paston School in North Walsham and at Cambridge University. He was also descended from John Rolfe. In the seventeenth century, Rolfe had married Pocahontas, the Native American princess beloved of his friend John Smith in Virginia, and had brought her back from colonial America to England, where she died tragically at the start of her journey home to the New World.

The parson's wife Frances Elwin came from a strict nonconformist background. For his part, Whitwell Elwin was of a Low Church persuasion, but as befitted a country gentleman of his time and place, he felt no call to fashionable evangelicalism. He followed a conservative path in theological and ecclesiastical matters, though his second son Hastings Philip, also a clergyman but who died young, moved his father toward a greater tolerance of High Church ideas later in his life. Ordained in 1840, Elwin served for three years as chaplain to the Bath Workhouse in Somerset, and completed his training for the priesthood in that county as a curate in the parish of Hemington and Hardington. In 1849 his brother offered him the Booton living following the death of his cousin Caleb.

During his time in Somerset, he published his first article (1843, on a story by French author Elzéar Blaze) in the *Quarterly Review*. His second article (1847) was on Shakespeare, and marked the beginning of his work on English authors. He associated with the *Quarterly* until 1885, and was its fourth editor, from 1853 to 1860. He accepted this position reluctantly, and worked at first together with the incumbent editor John Gibson Lockhart. After the death of Lockhart in 1854, Elwin took the reins alone. Beneath his selective eye, the *Quarterly* maintained its literary standards and held to a moderate Conservative viewpoint in a relatively stable period in Victorian England. He seems to have been a good choice on Murray's part for the position at that time, as he succeeded in steering the journal steadily, tactfully, and impartially, if unambitiously, through a decade in which it lost much of its earlier polemical edge. This loss was due largely to the weakness and disarray of Conservative politics following the split in the turbulent 1840s between High Tory protectionists and liberal reformists over the question of Corn Law repeal.

An enthusiast of eighteenth-century English literature, Elwin wrote erudite, witty, and insightful pieces for the *Quarterly* on authors as illustrious as Thomas Gray, Lawrence Sterne, Oliver Goldsmith, James Boswell and Samuel Johnson (twice), Henry Fielding, and William Cowper. Johnson and Edmund Burke – more for his style than his ideas – were two favourite authors. On his succeeding Lockhart, his first extensive essay was on Sterne. In 1854 he wrote his essay on Goldsmith as a quasi-review of John Forster's biography, though Elwin's piece stands as an independent assessment of Goldsmith's life and works. Forster, who introduced Elwin to Thomas Carlyle and Robert Browning, later edited *The Examiner* and is best known for his life of Dickens, a project to which Elwin made several contributions.

Elwin's preference for eighteenth-century literature, which he shared with other early luminaries of the *Quarterly* such as John Wilson Croker, suggests that his literary taste was rooted, like that of two of his fellow editors, in the old High Tory order of the aristocracy and landed gentry. The first editor, William Gifford, had been a narrow-minded seventeenth-century specialist. Croker and Lockhart, the third editor, had each launched fierce attacks on John Keats and Percy Shelley, despite Lockhart famously writing a life of his father-in-law Sir Walter Scott. But then Scott – unlike Keats, Shelley, or Leigh Hunt or William Hazlitt, two other Romantic authors attacked in the journal – was a 'Tory Romantic', as were William Wordsworth, Robert Southey, and later Benjamin Disraeli. The *Quarterly* thus had no problem in championing their work.

Though losing some of his passion for eighteenth-century works late in life, Elwin had little interest in the literature of his own time. Browning, George Eliot, and Alfred Tennyson failed to stir him; Matthew Arnold, Walter Swinburne, and Dante Gabriel Rossetti were barely on his radar. Nonetheless, he wrote articles for the *Quarterly* on several contemporary authors. He edited the works and letters of Robert Southey in 1850 and 1856 respectively. His lukewarm 1852 piece on Wordsworth provoked a strong reaction from readers. Perhaps his best review was on George Borrow (1857), an author whom Elwin knew personally and whose settings he understood, since Borrow was a Norwich native. Borrow's novels *Lavengro* and *Romany Rye* owed much to his first-hand experience of the gypsies who were encamped on Mousehold Heath above the city. Elwin admired William Makepeace Thackeray, and his review of that author's 1854 novel *The Newcomes* briskly countered a hostile review in *The Times*.

In estimating Elwin's contribution to the *Quarterly*, we should remember that in his day literary criticism remained largely the province of a community of gentleman-scholars like himself, who wrote for the rapidly expanding and financially remunerative market of newspapers and periodicals. This criticism formed part of a broader discourse of informed commentary on moral, social, and political issues. Despite the monetary rewards on offer, these men of letters saw themselves as responding to a quasi-religious calling; their literary criticism, didactic and lofty in tone, was perceived as a moral and spiritual as well as an aesthetic undertaking. Carlyle, in 1851, boldly saw it thus: 'Men of Letters are a perpetual Priesthood, from age to age, teaching all Men that God is still present in their life .... In the true Literary Man, there is thus ever, acknowledged or not by the world, a sacredness.' It was only after Arnold and George Saintsbury late in the century that the critical baton began to pass from the hands of these amateurs (albeit remunerated handsomely) into those of professional writers and academics.

The world of the gentleman's club played an important part in this literary and intellectual culture. In particular, the Athenaeum Club, which had been founded by Croker in 1824, aimed primarily to bring literati, artists, and scientists together in an atmosphere of enlightened sociability. The Athenaeum also welcomed men of the cloth, and in 1871 Elwin was elected by a vote of the membership. However he used the club rarely, spending most of his time in London at the offices of the *Quarterly* at John Murray's Albemarle Street premises or else at his lodging in Old Hummums Hotel.

Travelling usually by train, Elwin enjoyed his typical ten-day London excursions to the full and, being affable and humorous by nature, was deemed good company to one and all. Similarly, he enjoyed being the occasional weekend guest at the country seats of aristocratic friends like Lords Brougham and Westmorland, but was eager then to retreat to the bucolic tranquillity of the Norfolk countryside. Frances, who homeschooled their five children, anyway was a good intellectual foil to Elwin. Another part of his keenness to return home came from his sense of clerical duty; sometimes he would rush back to Booton on Saturday to perform Sunday services, only to return to London early on a Monday morning.

His editor's salary and contributor's fees from the *Quarterly* meant little to him, even though they provided a welcome boost to his clerical income; he rejected Murray's offer of £200 per annum to stay in London. As sociable as he was, Elwin deep down was a reclusive man with no aspiration to wealth, celebrity, or ecclesiastical preferment. In an 1843 letter to his sister Mary he wrote, 'I can only be happy in peace and retirement', and to the countess of Westmorland in 1857, 'I know too well how much happiness depends upon domestic quiet ever to be tempted to leave my present secluded nook.' Sarah Austin, wife of the jurist John Austin and daughter of Dr John Taylor, a transplanted Lancastrian who became a leading cultural light in Norwich, wrote of Elwin that he is 'a man of great wit and sense, imbued with generous and humane ideas' and that 'his is an existence difficult to describe to a foreigner'.

Yet he was not bereft of creative and educated company in his isolated home. Several notable figures occasionally left the big cities to seek him out in his rural eyrie: Scott, Murray, Forster, the poet Lord Robert Lytton and the liberal theologian 'Dean' Stanley of Westminster were among his visitors at Booton. Forster recalled a typically warm welcome from his host despite the austere surroundings. Anthony Trollope, Dickens, and Thackeray (a recollection of whom Elwin left unfinished) were friends; Thackeray called him 'Dr Primrose' after Goldsmith's well-intentioned but naïve parson in his 1766 novel *The Vicar of Wakefield*. Elwin is also more notoriously remembered as the manuscript reader who recommended that Murray reject Charles Darwin's *On the Origin of Species* on the grounds of insufficient evidence, and further that Murray encourage the author instead to write a popular book on pigeons.

In 1852 Murray published Elwin's selection of writings by Lord Byron, though the volume did not carry his name. In 1860, after having hesitated for several years, Elwin resigned his editorship of the *Quarterly* and turned his attention to furthering Croker's unfinished edition of Alexander Pope's works. However, he made it clear that he had agreed to undertake this task only out of respect for Croker's dying wish. Tiring of London and no longer obliged to go there regularly, he stayed more at home, and brought out two volumes of Pope's poems and three volumes of his letters from 1870 to 1874. Fatigued also by this task, in 1878 he turned over the remaining five-volume project to William John Courthope, who went on to become professor of poetry at Oxford University and to write one of the first critical-historical accounts of English poetry, in addition to a life of Addison.

Already in 1860, in Elwin's *Quarterly* essay on Cowper, we get a foretaste of hostility to Pope that may seem strange given his years of dedication to the new edition of the Augustan author's work. In praising Cowper's translation of Homer – written in blank verse and deeply respectful of the original text – as 'a great performance', Elwin, despite several reservations, is able to disparage Pope's earlier and more borrowed effort, in which 'puerile conceits, extravagant metaphors, and modern tinsel had been substituted for the majesty and simplicity of the Grecian'. And though Elwin reserved his severest criticism for the man rather than his poetry, he considered only a few works – *The Rape of the Lock*, *The Epistle of Eloisa to Abelard*, *The Dunciad*, and some sections of the *Satires* – to merit serious attention. 'The truth', he wrote to Murray, 'is that very much of Pope's verse is commonplace.' Elwin's caustic introduction to the edition – he considered Pope to be an eager and systematic fraudster; a lying, paranoid, malicious, self-serving rotter, pure and simple – as well as his voluminous critical apparatus threatened to overwhelm the whole undertaking and raised many eyebrows. Anxious over the probable chilly reception of Elwin's unfashionable opinion, Murray pleaded for moderation, but Elwin – always one to stick to his guns – retorted that the language of his appraisal of Pope was 'tame' compared with that of Thomas de Quincey. As someone who chose to live well out of the limelight and by basic principles of honesty and integrity, Elwin considered Pope's all too visible 'deceit' and 'delinquencies' to have been part of his personal undoing. In the introduction to Pope, he composes a sentence that is not out of place today in judging the snares of celebrity: 'The scrutiny to which the lives of celebrated men are subjected is one of the severest penalties they pay for fame.' And his moral indignation wins out over any artistic admiration: 'I do not pretend to think that genius is an extenuation of rascality.'

Aware of his growing physical limitations, Elwin abandoned an edition of Boswell's *Life of Johnson*. But he tried his hand at writing biography, with a brief life of Forster (1888), prefixed to the catalogue of the Dyce and Forster Library in the South Kensington (later Victoria and Albert) Museum in London. Elwin destroyed most of his papers and letters, but some of his voluminous correspondence – stylish but with a tone of warmth and spontaneity – survived in the hands of others. He dabbled in poetry of an unadventurous kind. He was a meticulous writer to the point of endless corrections, revisions, and elaborations; his finely wrought rhetorical turns often tended to be fastidious. Prone to procrastinate, his best and most concise prose was produced at speed, like that of his hero Johnson, often with looming deadlines. By all accounts, he was an unusually fine conversationalist, and possessed considerable oratorical skills, though he cared not for public speaking.

Partly to lift his sagging spirits following the deaths of his son Hastings Philip in 1874 and his only daughter Frances from tuberculosis in 1875, Elwin began to redesign and then rebuild his crumbling Perpendicular-style church, work that was completed in 1891. As a prelude to the reconstruction he had reseated the chancel in 1867, and had also shown his knowledge of church architecture as a consultant to the Dean and Chapter on the restoration of Norwich Cathedral. Moreover, as a gentleman stipendiary in a convenient living and as a member of the Booton manorial family, he had the means to do so. And in the mid-1890s he took over the running of the manor from his absentee brother Hastings. At no time therefore in this parish was there any risk, unlike in other rural communities, of conflict between clergyman and lord of the manor over the practice of religious life, as in the fierce battle of wits nearby between the evangelistic vicar William Wayte Andrew and the Huguenot-descended squire Sir John Boileau at Ketteringham, 15 or so miles to the south of Booton. Drawing on their diaries, the historian Owen Chadwick (*Victorian Miniature*, 1960) memorably brings to life the struggle between these two men for the minds of the local populace.

In belonging to the society of country gentry, Elwin shared Sarah Losh's status in the community and the privileges it afforded. Like her too, he had no architectural training; he based his designs for the new St Michael the Archangel on his own imagination and on details of other churches, many of which he visited. As models, he took Glastonbury Abbey for the west door; Lichfield Cathedral (possibly gesturing to Johnson) for the trefoil window above the chancel arch; St Stephen's Chapel in the Palace of Westminster for the west window, the glass for which was paid from Forster's uncancelled bequest of £1,500 to Elwin's late daughter; Temple Balsall, Warwickshire, for the nave windows; and Skelton, Yorkshire, for the priest's door. Furthermore, the pinnacled towers are close in style to the more fanciful 'gothick' of some eighteenth-century domestic architecture, as typified by Horace Walpole's Strawberry Hill and William Beckford's Fonthill Abbey.

Up in the north-west of England, Losh had realized her dream of spiritual exuberance by designing and building her church (completed in 1841) in what was, for the early years of Anglo-Catholic architectural fervour, a decidedly unconventional and eclectic mix of romantic interior design and Romanesque-Norman exterior forms. Later, down in the east of England, Elwin did much the same at Booton, rebuilding his church broadly within the dominant neo-Gothic Revival style (somewhere between Early English and Decorated), yet tweaking that orthodoxy with some highly personal flourishes both inside and out. To be fair, Augustus Pugin, the leading theorist of that style, favoured an interpretive medievalism, and so eagerly anticipated a 'carnival of architecture' to follow his polemical texts *Contrasts* (1836) and *True Principles of Pointed or Christian Architecture* (1841). These two books inspired John Ruskin to popularize a revival which dominated ecclesiastical and public architecture for the rest of the century. Pugin died in 1852, but I suspect he might have approved of Elwin's whimsical confection.

This shock of the not quite so old grows when, across the fields to the north of Booton, silhouetted against the vast sky of this mainly flat land, one catches sight of two of the most imposing medieval Perpendicular churches in England: St Agnes, Cawston, whose hammerbeam nave roof was, for Sir Gilbert Scott, doyen of the neo-Gothic revival, the finest in the land; and St Peter and St Paul, Salle, proud and lonely in its rural isolation, a reminder of the East Anglian worsted wool industry whose riches made possible the building of such impressive places of worship and centres of village life.

Located within a few miles of these two magnificent edifices, Elwin's church would seem at first to be no more than a young pretender. Some may even consider it a vulgar attempt to graft an inappropriate neo-Gothic model onto this ancient, unspoiled landscape. I rather felt that way on first acquaintance, but it has grown on me with each successive visit and with my better understanding of the man behind it. The exterior presents itself to the unsuspecting eye as a kind of exotic hallucination of turreted forms: pinnacles along the walls; two diagonally placed narrow towers at the western end each surmounted by crocketed pinnacles; a single three-tiered minaret set on the western gable between those twin towers. Unusually high doors add to this sensation of vertical idiosyncrasy. Of the diagonal placing of the towers, Sir Nikolaus Pevsner wrote that it 'is a conceit one would expect to find in 1820 rather than 1890'. One may delight in imagining a meeting of the minds between Whitwell and Sarah: Elwin's church displays the same unbridled romanticism that inspired Losh at Wreay.

The interior is an equally unconventional and finely wrought version of the contemporary style. Wooden doors, pews, stalls, and panelling are all exquisitely crafted throughout the church. Going against the predominant Gothic grain, there are no gloomy reminders of sin and judgement here, for this is Elwin's own vision of heaven. He wrote in 1876 to his lifelong friend Miss E. A. Holley, the daughter of a neighbouring parson, 'the trials and sufferings are transitory, the joys are lasting: … the language of the building should be in keeping with the enduring characteristic…. The aspect of a church should be to calm the worshipper, and raise him above the disturbances of earth into the peacefulness of heaven.'

As for the hammerbeam roof, loosely inspired by the church at Trunch in North-East Norfolk, which Elwin had known as a child, it is guarded by a double row of huge wood-carved angels suspended like giant bats. These are the work of a local master carver, James Minns, who also designed the enduring bull's-head emblem for the Colman's mustard company of Norwich. Booton is a fine example of the 140-plus angel roofs surviving in Great Britain. Most date from the fourteenth century and almost two-thirds may be found in the adjacent counties of Norfolk and Suffolk. Elwin's contribution to this form of artistic woodworking was yet another facet of his conscious return to medieval sources.

In the chancel, nave, and vestry, sets of stained-glass windows complete the representation of a celestial scene. Undertaken initially from 1880 to 1900 by the London firm of Cox, Sons & Buckley, and doubtless with specific theological themes in view, some of the windows – especially those in the nave done later by Alex Booker, a Royal Academician who worked for the firm at one time – simply become multiple celebrations of Elwin's vision. They display a joyful procession of biblical figures, most notably a host of enraptured angels singing and playing various musical instruments. As Sir John Betjeman put it, in a poem on Booton written for his 1974 BBC television series *A Passion for Churches*, 'No painful crucifixions here. / The heavenly choir, in Victorian dress, / Makes joyful music unto the Lord of Hosts.' Elwin's revivalism here is exact, as the angelic host had figured strongly in original Gothic design and in early Renaissance art. Moreover, the High Anglicanism of the Victorian age placed a strong emphasis on music, which for late-century aestheticism, sharply on the rise as the rebuilt church neared completion, was the ideal art to the condition to which, as Walter Pater famously pronounced, all others should aspire. The angels are represented as a bevy of 'heavenly creatures', a gathering of adolescent girls rendered more naturalistic, by way of a brightly hued surface-painting technique, than the willowy, brooding, and mysterious young women of the Pre-Raphaelites, whose revival of the deep brilliance of medieval 'flashed' pot-metal stained glass, exemplified by the work of Sir Edward Burne-Jones, was apparently not at all to Elwin's taste.

By contrast, the body language and facial expressions of the Booton angels are ingenuous and appealing in an altogether more wholesome, rustic way. They were modelled by some of Elwin's young female friends whom, perhaps slightly in the dubious manner of Lewis Carroll, he called his 'blessed girls'. His wife was not overly keen on these friendships, but tolerated them. Some of these young women were unpretentious locals, but others were higher born, and his relationships with the latter return us to Elwin's social place amid the upper class of English society and its literary-minded offspring. Two of them accompanied him on his tours of churches in search of inspiring designs. He engaged in intimate yet proper correspondence with Miss Holley for half a century; and, for ten years until she married the famous architect of Imperial India, Sir Edwin Lutyens, with Emily, daughter of Robert Lytton and granddaughter of the novelist Sir Edward Bulwer-Lytton. The Bulwer-Lytton family, like that of Walpole, had Norfolk roots; the Walpole seat, Houghton Hall, in grand Palladian style, lies only 20 miles or so north-west of Booton. One of his girls, possibly Emily or her eldest sister Betty, the first of the 'blessed girls', subsidized his church project, contributing a very large sum of money by the standards of today. Thirteen years old when their correspondence began and with fifty-eight years between them, Emily wrote about her epistolary friendship with Elwin in *A Blessed Girl: Memoirs of a Victorian Girlhood Chronicled in an Exchange of Letters, 1887–98* (1953). She mentions her father writing of Elwin as 'one of the last true men of letters left to us', referring to a dying breed of critics possessing 'scholarship, style, tenderness, discrimination, a vast knowledge of books' and pointedly, 'unlimited leisure'.

A man who wrote, preached, and built (he also designed his Elizabethan-style rectory, the village schoolhouse, and a new manor house), who was one of a number of 'eccentric incumbents' (in Betjeman's phrase from his 1943 BBC radio talk 'Oh to be in England'), Elwin died suddenly while dressing on the morning of 1 January 1900, aged 83. He had lost his wife less than two years earlier. As a defining statement of a nineteenth-century man, his timing early on that dawning day of a new century was impressive.

Hanging in the south end of the church (and accompanying this essay) is associate Royal Academician Henry Weigall's 1876 portrait of Elwin at 59, the rector's gift to his wife. It shows him looking cheerful and amenable, and barely suggests a man capable of a fantastic vision. But the church he built *is* fantastic, and every bit as much of an individualistic alternative to standardized design as is Sarah Losh's remarkable 'Lombardic' structure at Wreay. Lutyens described Booton as 'very naughty but built in the right spirit'. No longer used for worship, St Michael the Archangel is a listed building maintained by the Churches Conservation Trust. Its open-mouthed visitors form a new congregation able to feast their eyes on Elwin's bizarre, unlikely, but ultimately wondrous vision of his love of God.

Elwin's two surviving sons were both High Church clergymen. Warwick became a vicar at Worthing in Sussex; Edward became a Cowley Father missionary in India. Warwick wrote a lengthy memoir of his father, which he included in his 1902 two-volume edition of revised versions of Elwin's major essays under the title of *Some XVIII Century Men of Letters*. But the literary connection at Booton did not stop there, and was revived remarkably by another man of the cloth. As rector of Booton from 1935 to 1971, the Reverend Willis Feast, who had read English at Cambridge University in the 1920s, was an amateur poet whose tweed-suited figure, booming voice, and uninhibited interpretation of his spiritual vocation made him a minor celebrity in the Norwich alternative literary scene of the late 1960s and early 1970s. I recall his presence at exuberant poetry readings in old pubs such as the Adam and Eve and the Red Lion in Bishopsgate, close by the River Wensum and in the shadow of the cathedral spire.

Later in the 1970s a major celebrity, the writer and actor Stephen Fry, in between spells at boarding schools, lived at Booton House, a Victorian residence close to Elwin's church which his family had acquired in 1965. His father was a physicist and inventor, with something of a 'mad scientist' reputation among locals. From his reminiscences in *Moab Was My Washpot* (1997), it seems that Fry retains little affection for the time he spent there as a troubled and lonely teenager, before finding his vocation in considerable style during the following decade. The writerly connection survives at Elwin's old rectory, now the home of a retired philosophy professor whose field of study is logical and critical thinking, and who has authored books on those subjects. Looking out benevolently from his portrait in Booton church onto the paths trodden by his successors, I imagine Elwin approving of their contributions to that hive of literary activity he initiated in the tiny, sleepy Norfolk village one and three-quarter centuries ago.

4

A cultivating pen: Vita Sackville-West

Television has made celebrities out of chefs and gardeners. The moving image lends itself perfectly to representing the methods and techniques of cooking food and growing plants. An added value is the aesthetic pleasure the viewer derives from experiencing the personality of the celebrity narrator as well as the various shapes and colours of food or plants. The only senses that remain unengaged are those of touch and smell, though Aldous Huxley long ago had us believe that 'feelies' are not far away. Meanwhile, sound and vision are tantalizing enough to satisfy the viewer.

Before television came along, radio had the same function for gardening, if not as yet for cookery. The successful programme depended both on the host's expertise and their distinctive voice, their aural aura. Blessed with both qualities, Vita Sackville-West was one of the first British celebrity gardeners. Her media were radio and literature, her gardening books as eagerly awaited as her broadcasts. Even today, gardening (and cookery) books remain important commercial items, though now invariably as tie-ins to successful television series. Along with her contemporary C. H. Middleton, Sackville-West paved the way for such male gardening celebrities as Percy Thrower, Alan Titchmarsh, and Monty Don. She also set the stage for the female gardener closest in social profile and horticultural vision to herself, the dowager marchioness of Salisbury, formerly Mollie Wyndham-Quin and author of *A Gardener's Life* (2007). Lady Salisbury created imaginative (and well ahead of her times) organic gardens at her family seats, first at Cranborne Manor in Dorset, and later at Hatfield House in Hertfordshire, where she restored its sadly neglected plots in a design apposite to the house's seventeenth-century origin.

Ironically, though Sackville-West's greatest ambition was literary, at least until a certain disillusionment set in during her later life, we remember her best today for the garden of her home at Sissinghurst Castle in Kent, which she created with her husband and fellow author Harold Nicolson. First opened to the public in 1938, the garden already reflected their individual personalities fused into a shared overall vision. The home and garden, in the possession of the National Trust since 1967, have become a much-visited site. The fame of the garden lies in its imaginative layout, the result of a felicitous balance of Harold's austere, linear designs and Vita's organic and often impulsive approach to planting. He was the classicist, she the romantic. As she wrote in 1958, 'sweet disorder ... has to be judiciously arranged'. Their garden also mirrors the nature of their marriage: open, challenging, compromising, and enduring.

Vita Sackville-West as a married woman

Born into the English aristocracy in 1892, Vita was a social celebrity long before her forays into literature or gardening. In her childhood and youth, the family was often in the public eye. Her mother, Lady Victoria Sackville, provided great copy to the press, which lapped up two high-profile trials involving the succession and legacy of the family. Royalty paid visits to the palatial family seat at Knole in Kent. Vita gave her first press interview in 1911 at the tender age of 19, and much to her embarrassment Lady Sackville acted as a self-appointed publicist of her daughter's work.

Documented as highly and often as salaciously were Vita's marriage to Harold and her extramarital affairs with persons of both sexes. *Portrait of a Marriage*, Nigel Nicolson's 1973 book about his parents, included the posthumous publication of Vita's confessions of a drawn-out and tempestuous affair with Violet Trefusis. It gets better, or worse, depending on your view: Alice Keppel, Violet's mother, was King Edward VII's mistress. Vita attended his funeral and the coronation of his successor, George V. Victoria Glendinning's 1983 biography of Vita was instrumental in restoring a balance between her personal history and her twin careers as writer and gardener. Yet, in his 2014 biography *Behind the Mask*, Matthew Dennison swung the pendulum back towards her sexual notoriety, an unfortunate if unsurprising turn given our culture's appetite for titillation of that kind.

Whichever aspect of Vita's character appeals most to the reader – socialite, bisexual, gardener, writer – she was undoubtedly a complex human being. She wanted to have all or nothing. She could be cold and snobbish or warm, loyal, and sincere. At times she was obsessed by her creative side, but we expect that attribute of a true artist sitting at her desk or kneeling beside her flower beds. In both domains she was industrious and enterprising; the indolence of privilege (or privilege of indolence) was foreign to her nature. As a young woman, she embraced her expected social role with its round of parties, balls, and dinners, but already by the late 1920s she had begun to retreat from the charivari of London life and its literary rivalries. In a striking metaphor of rebirth through drowning, the first lines of her 1930 poem 'Sissinghurst' reveal both a disillusionment with the life she had been leading and a desire to lose herself in her newly acquired property: 'A tired swimmer in the waves of time / I throw my hands up: let the surface close: / Sink down through centuries to another clime, / And buried find the castle and the rose.' Eventually taking this retreat to the limit, she gave herself over to gardening and writing, as plain Vita Sackville-West rather than as Lady Nicolson, a title that discomfited her. In those twin activities she found the ideal marriage of form and function that she had glimpsed in 'Sissinghurst': 'Beauty, and use, and beauty once again / Link up my scattered heart, and shape a scheme / Commensurate with a frustrated dream.' In 1958, she wrote that her 'golden group' of cinquefoil, yarrow, and meadow-rue gave her 'more pleasure than all the nuggets in the cellars of the Bank of England'.

In a similar way to Karen Blixen and her colonial cronies, Vita had a dream – more available to the rich and privileged – of being 'splendid and dauntless and free', she and her kind belonging to a 'fraternity of adventurers' for whom a certain abandon was at once due to and a reaction to the circumstances of her upbringing. And like Blixen, she accomplished an American lecture tour in 1933, an activity that from Victorian times onward was a true mark of celebrity status. On return from America, she expressed her growing dislike of public life in a diary-poem that opens, 'Days I enjoy are days when nothing happens, / When I have no engagements written on my block, / When no one comes to disturb my inward peace, / When no one comes to take me away from myself.'

Had Vita confined herself to being a celebrity gardener, her writing would still have constituted a distinctive body of work. Her first gardening article appeared in the London *Evening Standard* in 1924, and by 1933 she was giving talks on BBC radio which were reproduced in *The Listener* magazine. *Country Notes* (1938) was an unofficial manifesto of her horticultural philosophy, while from 1946 to 1961 she contributed influential weekly columns to the *Observer* that confirmed her gardening expertise. To one reader in 1958, who perceived her as an armchair gardener, her retort was brisk and to the point, assuring him that 'for the last forty years of my life I have broken my back, my finger-nails, and sometimes my heart, in the practical pursuit of my favourite occupation'. And when not out in her garden, she stuck assiduously to her desk to produce five gardening books in the course of that decade, an output that led the American press to dub her as 'England's rose queen'.

In this regard, we may see that what inspires writing, and what writing demands of its serious practitioner, is comparable to the combined passion and discipline that goes to make up the 'compleat' gardener. Nigel Nicolson observes that for both his parents their garden was an accompaniment to their books. He adds that, when alone, Vita would 'garden all day, and write half the night'. Their first garden project was as newlyweds in Constantinople in 1913–14 when Harold took a diplomatic posting there, and it prompted them to pursue their hobby on buying Long Barn, their home in Kent, in 1914, where they lived until removing to Sissinghurst in 1932.

As Vita grew more enthusiastic for writing and gardening, she felt the influence of several pioneering woman gardener-authors. These included Elizabeth von Arnim, Winifred Fortescue, and especially Gertrude Jekyll, the magisterial female gardener of Vita's young adulthood, whose house and garden at Munstead, in Surrey, she had first visited in 1917 accompanied by her mother and the famous architect Edwin Lutyens (he of the Elwin-Lytton connection in Chapter 3). Meanwhile, across the Atlantic, in Lenox, Massachusetts, Edith Wharton, who thought herself to be a better landscape gardener than novelist, had published *Italian Vistas* in 1904. In the same way as Vita, but with a contrasting routine which afforded her more time for socializing, Wharton divided whole days between writing early on and gardening later in the day. Though she delighted in a 'mass of bloom', she cared not for the controlled wildness of the English country style, preferring what was, for some, an all too perfect Italianate model at The Mount, her home in the Berkshire hills of western Massachusetts. For Wharton, to a greater extent than for Sackville-West, the relationship between house and garden was all-important. And her gardening prowess meant as much to her as her literary success, since she compared the number of her first prizes at flower shows with the number of weeks her novel *The House of Mirth* spent at the top of the *New York Times* bestseller list.

Dennison's view is that the Long Barn and Sissinghurst gardens cohere aesthetically rather more than do Vita's uneven novels, or her biographies, which though professionally written seem to exist outside of her personality. He adds that she was an *amateur* gardener and so felt less pressure to prove herself than she did as a professional writer. Ironic, then, that for many today her garden is the main proof of her imaginative mind and creative talent. Yet her dedication to gardening was comparable to, even indissociable from, that which she put into her writing. If one is serious about these arts, then they require determination, perseverance, and sheer graft in addition to imaginativeness, sensitivity, patience, nimbleness, and attention to detail. And they also require careful planning, if they are to make sense and succeed as artifacts. As Robert Pogue Harrison writes in *Gardens: An Essay on the Human Condition* (2008), 'like a story, the garden has its own developing plot, as it were, whose intrigues keep the caretaker under more or less constant pressure'. Little wonder, then, that – like Vita – 'every "real" gardener is by nature obsessive'.

After a day of rain, the Kentish skies cleared to usher in a perfect May morning as I made my long-awaited first visit to Sissinghurst. Having duly followed the crowd along the borders of Vita and Harold's colour-coded garden, I climbed the tower in which Vita had made her study. In an alcove off the spiral staircase, I listened to a recording of her reading 'Sissinghurst'. Its beauty reminded me that she remains underestimated as a poet and always overshadowed in a literary sense by her close friend, if very different kind of writer, Virginia Woolf, to whom she dedicated that particular poem.

Knole has a Poet's Parlour, and Vita began writing at the age of 12 partly to offset a lonely childhood as an only child in a rambling stately home. A verse drama, *Chatterton*, was her first book, self-published in 1909 with a print run of 100 copies. It represented the start of a long literary career in fiction, nonfiction, and poetry. Her first novel, *Heritage* (1919), was a success, while *The Dragon in Shallow Waters* (1921) initially outsold D. H. Lawrence's *Women in Love*. It would be less than magnanimous, however, to compare the subsequent sales figures of those works, for who remembers Vita's book today? Such are the vagaries of literary reputation. Moreover, not everyone found her writing to their taste; Ronald Firbank (but who remembers him?) lampooned her romantic and near-caricatured characters, settings, and plots. Besides, Vita was acutely self-critical, her popularity as a novelist failing at least outwardly to impress her. Of her novels, she claimed to like only *Seducers in Ecuador* (1924), curiously enough a book written at great speed in more ways than one (benzedrine was the fashionable upper of the day) and in a popularized Bloomsbury style. That style hints perhaps at where her literary ambition was leading her. Yet she remained a popular novelist of a kind that was of no interest to the experimental high-mindedness of modernist peers like Woolf and Edith Sitwell. She had become a literary celebrity, and in 1928, like Karen Blixen later, she was invited to give a series of radio talks on literary subjects, an opportunity that was afforded her largely by her friendship with Hilda Matheson, the BBC's director of talks. Her performances continued until 1932, giving her a substantial taste of the microphone and of a new audience, and they paved the way for her broadcasts on gardening matters, a popular mouthpiece she shared for a short time with the doyen of celebrity gardeners, C. H. Middleton, whose programme *In Your Garden* may be said to have established the form.

In the late 1920s and early 1930s, Vita was at the peak of her powers as a novelist. *The Edwardians* (1930) and *All Passion Spent* (1931), a *roman à clef* about her affair with Violet Trefusis, are the two works of fiction for which she is best remembered. Leonard Woolf thought the latter to be her best novel. Though subsequent works, like *Family History* (1932) and *The Dark Island* (1934), continued to sell well, they showed signs of declining quality. Virginia Woolf thought the latter to be too personal, much more so than *All Passion Spent*. By 1942, the edgy *Grand Canyon* could not find a publisher in either Leonard Woolf or William Heinemann; it was accepted eventually by Michael Joseph.

During that most productive period of the late 1920s and early 1930s, Vita was also at her best as a poet, though this side of her literary career is now barely remembered. And she cared much more about reaction to her poetry than to her fiction. Even in her day – to her great chagrin, for her dream was to be a poet of stature – she went relatively unnoticed. She wrote some very good poems in an old-fashioned style, but never received the recognition she craved. Nonetheless *The Land* won the conservative Hawthornden Prize in 1927, despite Virginia Woolf failing to take it seriously and both Edith Sitwell and Rebecca West disliking it. This long, highly schematic exercise in the neo-georgic overflows with conscious archaisms, but it is an extraordinary achievement for all that in capturing the essence of traditional English rural life and landscape. It was revived as a morale booster during the Second World War in connection with the 'Dig for Victory' campaign to which Middleton's radio talks made a major contribution.

By the early 1940s, Vita found herself increasingly marginalized as a poet. Though she participated in Edith and Osbert Sitwell's 1943 reading at the Aeolian Hall, she was not invited to read at a similar event at the Wigmore Hall later that year. Some critics and scholars (including Glendinning) deem *The Garden* (1946) better than *The Land*; her old nemesis Edith Sitwell praised it, and it won the Heinemann Prize. Yet it met with little success. Embarrassed by and extremely diffident about the poem, which she felt was outdated and a mere virtuoso exercise, Vita disdained it. It depressed her to the point of her being ready 'to devote all my energies to the garden, having abandoned literature'. Her acceptance of artistic limitation surfaces in the 'Spring' section of the poem: 'Small is our vision, rare the searchlight beam; / Few moments given but in truth supreme.' Other lines reveal her pessimism. In a 'Dedication' (to Katherine Drummond), she admits to

'Failing as gardener, failing as poet.' In 'The garden' section, which functions as a prologue, she refers to 'the gardener half artist [who] must depend / On that slight chance' beyond all planning. Other lines suggest nonetheless an unbroken faith in her adventurous spirit. In 'Summer', she reasserts a confident imperative: 'So let invention riot. Dare / Th' unorthodox; be always bold; ... No prudent prose, but lyric rhetoric.' Having begun 'Spring' by quoting four lines from *The Waste Land*, beginning with 'April is the cruellest month', she strikes a positive Eliotian note in the 'Autumn' section: 'Enlarging vision slowly turns the key / And swings the door wide open on the long / Vistas of true significance.' Despite many doubts, she had clearly not forsaken her quest for transcendent language.

Vita and Harold existed on the fringe of the Bloomsbury group, sharing some of its aesthetic sophistication and bohemian attitudes if not its rigorous intellectualism. Both were sensitive, highly intelligent, and well read, but equally they were practical individuals in a way that few, if any, of the Bloomsbury coterie were. Bloomsbury viewed Vita and her family circle as relics of the Edwardian era, steeped too deeply in Establishment tradition, protocol, and conservative taste to be capable of truly radical or progressive ideas and their expression. Vita failed Bloomsbury's test of intellectuality, urbanity, and avant-gardism. In Virginia Woolf's mind, Vita had 'all the supple ease ... not the wit'. Yet, Virginia modelled *Orlando* on Vita's bisexuality, while the unconventional sexual life of the Bloomsbury group held nothing over Vita's own enterprise in that respect. For her part, Vita found herself both demoralized and inspired by Virginia's literary talent, and she realized that she might try to emulate if not match her. Then again, notwithstanding her fragile genius, Virginia was neither gardener nor socialite. Vita was both, in spades, as it were, and a distinctive writer too. If ever there was a celebrity on several fronts, then she was an extraordinary example of one.

George Barker as a young man

5

Modern romantics:
Dylan Thomas and George Barker

Dylan Thomas and George Barker were true contemporaries whose personal backgrounds and literary careers ran much on parallel lines, and their similarities considerably outweigh their differences. Both left school early and were largely self-taught, though Thomas completed a secondary school education at Swansea Grammar under the gaze of his father, who taught English there. Thomas senior inculcated a taste for the sound as much as the sight of literature in a precocious son who otherwise hated the institution. Both poets were anti-academic from an early age, sharing a deep-seated belief that academic criticism was incompatible with creativity. Though both were prime *épateurs du bourgeois*, they showed little social or political mindedness, a detachment unusual for poets budding in the 1930s. Thomas wrote, 'It's the poetry ... that counts, not ... continent, country, island, race, class, or political persuasion.'

Barker's *Calamiterror* (1937), written under the sign of Blake, Wordsworth, and Shelley, as war clouds gathered, insisted nonetheless on the moral imperative of the poet, while its ominous tone echoed Yeats in 'The second coming' rather than the more ideological line taken by W. H. Auden and his cohorts. Furthermore, *The True Confession of George Barker, Book One* (1950) appeared in the 'Key Poets' booklet series of a communist outfit, Fore Publications, though the publisher's broad outlook, which dismayed its more doctrinaire adherents, accounts for this work of philosophical subjectivism appearing on its list. Much later, *Anno Domini* (1983) carried an implicit critique of that decade's Thatcherite politics in the United Kingdom, but it was not Barker's way to be direct about such matters. Even so, in that volume, as a dedicated pleasure seeker living in rural retreat from the world at large, he could send himself up: 'in a time of hedonists and belly dancers / wise men draw the blinds and bolt the doors'.

Neither poet saw active service in the Second World War. Barker was mostly in the United States after a brief spell of teaching in Japan, and Thomas, who had been rejected for duty on grounds of physical unfitness, worked in the film industry and later at the BBC, where T. S. Eliot got him a radio job boosting national morale through cultural programming.

Both men had already decided anyway to live as poets alone. Totally dedicated to their vocation, they were literary mavericks for whom the play of words was everything. Barker was uninterested in self-promotion, fame, or adulation; by contrast, Thomas found them rather alluring, ultimately to his cost. According to critic, fellow poet, and fellow Norfolk resident Anthony Thwaite, Barker 'looked and sounded and behaved exactly as a poet should'. And Thomas's magnetic presence, as Karl Shapiro wrote in the mid-1950s, was already creating 'a general audience for a barely understandable poet'. Both were as excessive in their lives as in their verses. Serious drinkers and frequently in equally serious need of money, they could be arrogant, rude, and hurtful. Then again, they could be generous, tender, and charming. Their habitual booze-ups and related outbursts occasionally led to punch-ups, which in turn fed back into the myth of the impetuous, irresponsible poet. Yet they laboured under no illusions. They had known early on how they wished to spend their lives, had calculated the risks accordingly, and for the most part had not hesitated to take them.

They were not close friends but generally friendly rivals. In 1950, Thomas turned on Barker by attacking the easier target of his earlier work. Outlandish personality though he was, Barker by then simply could not match the phenomenal rise of Thomas's celebrity, especially as it reflected the popularity of the Welshman's radio work. Rather as Vita Sackville-West was caught in the shadow of Virginia Woolf in the 1920s and 1930s, Barker was sidelined by Thomas after the Second World War, though it is doubtful whether Barker, unlike Vita, cared too much one way or another, as he insouciantly maintained his own small circle of admirers and acolytes.

However, from a critical standpoint, both poets found themselves snubbed by the British literary establishment. This happened particularly under the sway of the Movement from the mid-1950s to the mid-1960s, a poetic turn that was antithetical to their expansive, rhetorical styles. In any case, both fiercely resisted appropriation by or membership of literary schools and movements. Neither were New Apocalyptics nor surrealists, though a surrealistic vein runs through some of their early verse and some of Thomas's prose. At best, both were a type of modern romantic, if ultimately unclassifiable by that or any other label. One fact is irrefutable: at the start of their careers, along with David Gascoyne, they were 'Parton Street poets' but only insofar as Daniel Archer, the proprietor of the London bookshop of that name, gave each his debut in print.

In their religious experience both men lapsed from the faith of their families: Barker was a Roman Catholic, Thomas a Protestant. Both were Celts – at least Barker half-so, a native Englishman whose Irish mother's side came out strongest in him as a literary tinker of sorts, footloose and fancy-free. Thomas saw himself more as an English poet from Wales than as a Welsh poet, and always, like his friend Vernon Watkins, dissociated himself from Welsh language, tradition, and community, a stance that accounts for an ambiguous Welsh response to him in his lifetime.

Swansea had been a seaside watering-hole for genteel English visitors since the late eighteenth century, and a sector of its population preserved those middle-class values. Thomas senior belonged to a generation of educated Welsh for whom 'aspiring' and 'anglicizing' were near interchangeable words. Dylan's elocution lessons ordered by his father earned him the nickname of 'Lord Cutglass', while his café-lounging with the other 'Kardomah Boys' was no more than typical of any youthful group of provincial British artistic wannabes. And he happily sent himself up. *Return Journey*, a nostalgic 1947 dramatic text, offers this self-portrait: 'a bombastic adolescent provincial bohemian with a thick-knotted artist's tie made out of his sister's scarf ... and a cricket shirt dyed bottle-green; a gabbing, ambitious, mock-tough, pretentious young man'. In his mainly prose piece *Reminiscences of Childhood* (1943), Thomas declared that that 'the sea-town was my world; outside a strange Wales, coal-pitted, mountained, river-run ... moved about its business which was none of mine'. As Roland Mathias wrote in *Poetry Wales* in 1974, 'He knew *about* Wales right enough ... but he hadn't been inside [its] tradition.'

Writing in 1983 on the two poet Thomases – Dylan and R. S. – C. B. Cox noted the irony of hostile English critics associating Dylan's verse with a stereotypical Welshness, while very little about him was consciously Welsh other than a love of the rural and maritime landscapes that inform some of his best poems. His critical fate was thus to be shot by both sides, his triumph to be talented enough to trump their objections. And in *Welsh Poets* (1946), Thomas distanced himself wittily from those fellow countrypeople who 'give the impression that their writing in English is only a condescension to the influence and ubiquity of a tyrannous foreign tongue'.

Thomas's appeal to me as an adolescent hungry for literary heroes lay in his unabashed love of language as well as in the emotional charge of his verse. 'Poem in October', for instance, with its rich imagery, rolling rhythms, and shapely stanzas, seemed to me to have it all. Its high voltage looked as good on the page as it sounded when read aloud. His attractiveness to a generation raised on rock and roll – and so to whom the pleasures of associated sight and sound went hand in hand – extended to his voice, his presence, and the hedonistic, if tragic, abandon of his way of life. In all but physical appearance, Thomas was a rock star *manqué*. No wonder the rock generation's own bard-in-chief, an exceptionally literate troubadour called Bob Dylan, took Thomas's first name as his own last one. Another poet of rock, John Lennon, attributed the influence of Thomas to his key decision to write lyrics to songs. While the literary critics and academics of the 1960s turned their backs on Thomas, the young rebels and would-be romantics of that decade's counterculture wholeheartedly embraced his full-on style in art and life alike.

Thomas was not naïve; he played his bardic role eagerly, cleverly, and to the limit. Relishing public eye and ear, he was instrumental in creating his own literary celebrity. Here was a poet whose name appeared in the newspapers, if more often for his uninhibited actions than for his verses alone. And his prose pieces, notably *Under Milk Wood* and *A Child's Christmas in Wales*, became part of mass culture via their radio exposure. Even my parents, intelligent but not literary individuals, knew Thomas's work. With so wide an audience, Thomas could afford to ignore most of the critical tirades directed at him.

Though the culture of Wales and the accent of its English seemed exotic to me as a born and bred easterner, when he wrote of Swansea in *Reminiscences of Childhood* as an 'ugly, lovely town', evoking its port and describing its topography, he reminded me of my own earliest years in my birthplace of Grimsby beside the cold, grey, exhilarating North Sea. His attachment to his western sea sparked an elemental kinship that transcended the differences between his and my own origins. Between Swansea and Grimsby, the accents might differ, but the daily round was much the same, one dominated by dock and ship, and by a motley landscape, mundane bustle, and local character typical of British provincial towns in both our boyhoods.

It is difficult to comprehend now that his first publication, *18 Poems*, which appeared late in 1934, was ignored. Undeterred, he began to be noticed two years later for *25 Poems*, a volume praised by Edith Sitwell. In 1940, riffing on Joyce in a homage to the value of verbal ingenuity, his collection of short stories *Portrait of the Artist as a Young Dog* opened him to a transatlantic readership for the first time. During wartime, he also became a celebrity of the airwaves. Wildly popular with audiences in sore need of uplifting entertainment, his prose readings kept him firmly in the public ear. Those performances gained much of their liveliness from his borrowing of the incantatory *hwyl* of Welsh preachers, proving that Thomas happily drew on Welsh tradition when it suited him to do so. He returned to his versifying in 1946 with *Deaths and Entrances*; he had composed most of it, however, before 1941.

His reputation reached new heights with the 1952 publication of *Collected Poems*. In three years it sold over 30,000 copies, a huge return for a volume of poetry, much of which is grasped with difficulty even by the trained reader. He first visited the United States in 1950, returned there in 1952 and twice in 1953. Despite the adulation, Thomas saw the underlying stress and insanity of his (and most others') American lecture tours, which he satirized gleefully and at his own expense in *A Visit to America,* written in the last year of his life: 'catarrhal troubadours, lyrical one-night-standers, dollar-mad nightingales, remittance-bards from at home, myself among them booming with the worst'.

Drinking killed the radio star. During his second tour in 1953, he died amid characteristic fanfare in New York City on 9 November, aged 39. On the first day of that fateful year 29-year-old Hank Williams, king of the Country and Western singers, the 'Hillbilly Shakespeare', equally flushed by fame and success in his own lyrical way, had died of too many pills and too much booze. The spell of both men's words and the magic of their voices had propelled each to prominence in their respective arts, but their identical lifestyles led to their early demises. Nonetheless, Thomas had shown his mettle as a performer, placing himself in the vanguard of literature for mass consumption. He thus anticipated the media-

Dylan Thomas photographed by Nora Summers, 1938

driven pop culture that exploded in the 1960s and would particularly appeal to younger consumers on radio, records, and eventually television too.

I may have first heard Thomas reading his work on a celebrated recording of the premiere of *Under Milk Wood* in New York City on 14 May 1953. The strangely resonant title; the eccentric characters with remarkable names; the nostalgic sense of place; the moods of earthy joy and lingering sadness; the subtle wit and mischievous humour; the dynamics of the readers' voices – all seemed to my impressionable young mind to offer a near-perfect whole. It wasn't, of course, but why spoil such an epiphany? Reading the part of Reverend Eli Jenkins, Thomas's litany of place-names as he recites the clergyman's poem (his 'morning service') on town and wood conjured up a very different Britain from the one I knew, yet spoke to me inspiringly of cultural and geographical variety. The fifteen curtain calls the show received on that first Manhattan airing suggest how universally resonant it was, its ragged edges as precious to its success as its peculiar vision. Published posthumously, the text represents the beginning of Thomas's unrealized career as a playwright, though structurally it is more an episodic narrative for voices than a conventional dramaturgical work. First broadcast in Britain in January 1954 with Richard Burton in the cast, *Under Milk Wood* serves for most of his audience as Thomas's grand epitaph, the creation for which he remains best known and liked despite it having been critically relegated to a list of his minor works.

His reputation in the realm of popular culture grew in the years following his death, but in the 1960s collapsed in the narrower eyes of the literary world. His last poems especially came under the hammer. Somes critics even claimed perversely that in rendering obscure his meanings, Thomas was wreaking a terrible Welsh vengeance on the language of the English colonizer. Others plainly derided his work, as John Wain puts it, for its 'open emotionalism, the large verbal gestures which seem to them mere rant, the rapt pleasure in elaborate craftsmanship, and above all the bardic tone'. For his admirers, however, these attributes were exactly what rendered his poetry honest and dazzling. Wain elsewhere tells the story of Robert Graves dismissing Thomas's poetry as 'meaningless gibberish' and offering a pound to anyone who could persuade him otherwise. Given his own rumbustious poet's life and self-exile from the mainstream, we might have expected Graves to have been more sympathetic to his peer. Even if few of Thomas's poems were readily comprehensible, there was always the irresistible power of his diction and rhythm. How could any young poetry enthusiast have resisted the sonic booms, flashing lights, and heartstring-tugs of 'Fern Hill' or 'Poem in October'?

Thomas enjoyed a brief revival of interest in the 1970s; thereafter his reputation declined again until 2014, the centenary of his birth, a year that brought him and his work back into the limelight. It also kickstarted a mainly Welsh initiative to reestablish Thomas in that pantheon in which he was once deemed by his vociferous American sponsors as 'the greatest living poet' in the English language.

❀❀❀

George Barker's career began brilliantly, with Eliot and Yeats, no less, singing his praises. Yeats called him 'the finest poet of his generation' and was reminded of Gerard Manley Hopkins by the rhythmical quality of his verse. Eliot's opinion of Barker as a 'genius' led to his being accepted by Faber, where Eliot was in charge of the poetry list. Barker's first volume, simply entitled *Poems*, appeared in 1935, while a year later his work appeared unsurprisingly in two major anthologies, the *Oxford Book of Modern Verse, 1892–1935*, edited by Yeats, and the *Faber Book of Modern Verse*, edited by Michael Roberts. Barker's star remained in the ascendant for the next twenty years. By the late 1940s, *Poetry Quarterly* ranked him along with Thomas and David Gascoigne as one of the three major poets of his generation, thus echoing Eliot's early encomium. Yet a persistent difficulty in finding a place for Barker in the lineage of English poetry began to arise during wartime, when he was tagged rather conveniently as a neo-romantic (along with poets such as W. S. Graham and Vernon Watkins) and quite inaccurately as a member of the short-lived New Apocalyptics along with Watkins, Henry Treece, J. F. Hendry, G. S. Fraser, and Nicholas Moore.

We may understand these mislabels as efforts to locate Barker among those poets reacting to the urbane sophistication and social consciousness of Auden and other 1930s modernists. While Auden's literary reputation nosedived in the explosive 1940s only to rebound strongly thereafter, Barker's did not. And unlike Thomas, whose level of popular exposure allowed his reputation in the 1950s to withstand a highbrow critical assault on the romantic strain in poetry, Barker's began to slide at a time when he was mainly disporting himself as a prize bohemian in various Soho drinking dens. His mystical, mythical, expansive, allusive verse increasingly fell out of style as a more contemporaneous and ironic style took center stage. Showcased by Robert Conquest's *New Lines* anthology (1956) and epitomized by the verse of Philip Larkin, this poetic turn was propped up firmly by an academically leaning literary establishment to which serious poetry meant cool control of the vernacular. Writers as teachers, or vice versa, were coming into vogue, and though Barker took visiting lectureships first in Japan and later in the United States, they were primarily a means of making generally meagre ends meet, and were never perceived by him as merely a steady prop to the spare-time pursuit of poetry. The idea of such a secure arrangement was anathema to Barker, as it was to Thomas.

Barker's reputation in Britain also suffered from his expatriate existence in Italy and the United States, and he continued to be neglected in the 1960s despite winning the Guinness Prize in 1962 for his ninth collection, *The View from a Blind I*, a title referring indirectly to a boyhood incident in which he had caused the loss of his younger brother Kit's left eye. As his biographer Robert Fraser puts it, 'by 1964 George Barker was an anomaly. He was a senior poet whose art continued to develop, but whom few of the young knew. He was a religious poet in a secular age, a significant figure in the history of twentieth-century British verse whom academics ignored.' His response to this indifference had been to hole up in Italy with two of his long-term partners, at first Dede Farrelly, then later Elspeth Langlands whom he finally married in 1989. Only after resettling in England with Elspeth in 1967 until his death in 1991 was he again reckoned with as a minor celebrity in the iconoclastic British poetry revival of that time, and again recognized as an important voice in the history of twentieth-century English poetry.

Barker anyway was a survivor – after all, he outlived Thomas by thirty-eight years – and while his national reputation never fully regained its early strength, a combination of factors brought him notice again: Robert Fraser's dedication to writing the life and editing the works of this 'chameleon poet'; a newfound status as a somewhat reluctant literary guru during almost a quarter-century of holding court in deepest Norfolk; and the sheer force of his mercurial personality. Herein lies a delicious irony. Notwithstanding the romantic, rebellious, and bardic qualities he shared with Thomas and with Whitmanesque poets like Allen Ginsberg, there was also an element of the neoclassicist about Barker. He disliked, for instance, what he had perceived as the overly casual and careless writing of the Beat Generation – and most American poetry, for that matter. In New York in 1958, he was poking fun at the forefathers of the hippie counterculture, especially Jack Kerouac for *On the Road*, yet he too functioned largely within that alternative scene in England in his later years.

I had discovered and begun to enthuse over Thomas's work as a schoolboy in the early 1960s, but I had paid no attention to Barker. He came into my purview when I found myself skirting a literary micro community over which he presided in the late 1960s and early 1970s. Tucked away in the narrow lanes of the north Norfolk countryside, the tiny village of Itteringham included among its residents during this time a number of writers. At Bintry House, a fine seventeenth-century brick and flint farmhouse overlooking the River Bure, which had been acquired with the financial help of Graham Greene, George and Elspeth Barker lived with their daughter Raffaella. Elspeth and Raffaella are novelists. Other poets were Maurice Carpenter, a former communist and Barker's old friend from the 1930s, who shared space at Bintry for a while; Derek Neville, who lived in the Mill House; and Sebastian Lockwood, who inhabited a small cottage. The poet Sebastian Barker is George's son by the Canadian poet Elizabeth Smart, with whom George had a lengthy and tempestuous affair beginning in the war years, and whose lyrical account of their relationship, *By Grand Central Station I Sat Down and Wept* (1945), later gained the status of a cult novel. Sebastian lived nearby in the small market town of Reepham; and Tristram Hull, co-founder with Martin Green of the literary magazine *Nimbus* in 1951, lived in another nearby village.

As a postgraduate student at the University of East Anglia in Norwich, I was also an occasional editor in 1969 of *Norch*, a cheaply and messily duplicated poetry magazine whose title was an affectionate take on local pronunciation of the city's name. The task of editing this roughhewn publication was shared by a small group of habitués of Bristow's Paperbacks, located in an alleyway opposite the Bridewell Museum and a focal point of the city's alternative scene. Though I never made it onto his guest list, several of my cronies attended Barker's well-oiled Saturday evening gatherings at Bintry House. These parties were notorious for exuberant displays of declamatory poetics and generally boisterous behaviour. Sebastian Lockwood, who lives now in an equally remote part of the Monadnock Mountains in New Hampshire, often acted as Barker's minder; on Sunday mornings he would accompany him on a drive to the beach at Sheringham where Barker nursed his hangover with a bracing dose of North Sea air. While the dust settled between those wild weekends, Barker got on with the serious business of writing poetry, and maintained an output of considerable quality which included several beautiful reflections, such as 'At Thurgarton Church' and 'Morning in Norfolk', on the age-old rural environment in which he had chosen to cocoon himself.

In 1973 Martin Green and John Heath-Stubbs, another of Barker's close friends, coedited *Homage to George Barker on His Sixtieth Birthday*. With contributions by Gascoigne, Ginsberg, Thwaite, Geoffrey Hill, G. S. Fraser, C. H. Sisson, and David Wright, it showed that Barker, despite his bucolic retreat, had not been forgotten by a substantial group of fellow poets and critics. The broader literary world, however, declined to join in. In the 1980s, the 'Martian School' of poets spearheaded by Craig Raine, then poetry editor at Faber, overlooked him; only Michael Schmidt recognized his work by publishing it in the influential *Poetry Nation Review*. Nonetheless, *Collected Poems* (1987) received much praise even when refracted in the Oxonian prism of John Bayley's prose; though Bayley, then Wharton Professor of English Literature, failed to cut any ice with an ever anti-academic Barker. In the same year, writer and broadcaster Melvyn Bragg got wind of renewed interest in Barker, and commissioned Irish colleague Carlo Gebler to direct an episode of London Weekend Television's arts flagship *South Bank Show* on him. It was hardly a return to his lionized 20s and 30s – Robert Fraser calls it a 'flicker of media attention' – but at least he and his poetry were revealed to a much wider audience.

As with Thomas, I like best reading Barker's poems aloud to get the full flavour of his subtle cadences and bold diction. Then, I feel I am in the company of a versatile and masterful poet, who can be both erudite and earthy, lofty and intimate, spiritual and sensual, flippant and deadly serious, sometimes all within a single poem. His is a kind of *vers chaud* of body and soul, the vehicle of an often-startling iconoclasm, of a making and breaking of myths, of a bold celebration of rhetorical skill harnessed to a strictness of form. Barker and Thomas may often frustrate even the most willing reader by their quirks of meaning, yet both poets may excite and mesmerize by the sonorous flow of their lines, the sheer beauty of their language, and the unquestionable depth of their feeling.

Ngugi wa Thiong'o, London, 2007

6

A mightier pen: Ngugi wa Thiong'o

In independence-era Africa, young James Ngugi seemed destined for literary celebrity on emerging as a promising young writer at the 1962 Conference of African Writers of English Expression held at Makerere College in Kampala, Uganda. This rather awkwardly named conference marked a watershed in the anglophone application of what Ngugi later called an 'Afro-European (or Euro-african) choice of our linguistic praxis'. All the heavy hitters attended: novelist Chinua Achebe, playwright and novelist Wole Soyinka, both from Nigeria; the poet Kofi Awoonor from Ghana; exiled South African author Lewis Nkosi; Langston Hughes, who travelled from the United States to represent black American litera-ture. I imagine Ngugi eagerly seeking out Achebe, deeming him the leading light in fiction based on precolonial and colonial history, and asking him to read the manuscripts of his own first two novels tracing that history in his native Kenya. At the same time Ngugi was making a name in Kenya as an opinionated jour-nalist, authoring around fifty op-ed pieces from 1961 to 1964. I also imagine him listening carefully to Nigerian scholar and activist Obi Wali's paper, 'The dead end of African literature', a timely lament for the absence of works in native African languages. Wali's putative call for change would have made Ngugi reflect further on what was lacking in his continent's literature, and on why this might be so.

Ngugi's own early politicization was thus reinforced at Makerere; it was later to be intensified by his exposure abroad to Frantz Fanon and Karl Marx. This steady formation fulfilled an ideological predisposition in the mind of the young writer stemming from his boyhood and youth. Born in Limuru near Nairobi in 1938, James Ngugi had moved from a colonial to a nationalist school where he began to understand the nature of Kenyan identity. He then witnessed members of his own family suffering and his home village burning down during the ruthless British repression of the Mau Mau uprising in the 1950s against its colonial rule.

His first two novels were published in England (*Weep Not, Child*, 1964; *The River Between*, 1965), by which time Ngugi had arrived at the University of Leeds to write a master's thesis on Caribbean literature. In gaining a schol-arship to Leeds, Ngugi followed in the footsteps of Soyinka, who had studied there from 1954 to 1960. However, Ngugi found himself devoting most of his time to writing *A Grain of Wheat*, the last part of an historical trilogy beginning with *Weep Not, Child*. Meanwhile, its second part, *The River Between*, was duly celebrated within the Leeds School of English and across the university as a whole. In completing his trilogy, Ngugi had emulated Achebe's own cycle of novels (*Things Fall Apart*, *No Longer at Ease*, *Arrow of God*) tracing the history of colonization and native resistance up to the threshold of *Uhuru*, or national independence.

'For Philip. Solidarity. NW Thiong'o', reads the penned inscription to my well-thumbed paperback copy of Ngugi's 1989 novel *Matigari*. It was April 1994; I was attending a conference devoted to Ngugi and organized at the Berks (county) campus of the Pennsylvania State University by African specialist and professor of English, Charles Cantalupo. At that time, I was his colleague in the Penn State English department but teaching at another of the university's multiple campuses. Part of the event included a book signing. I made the most of my brief turn in the line to tell Ngugi that I too had been a Leeds English student while he was there, and that we had lived in adjacent houses at Bodington Hall, a sprawling complex of student residences on the northern edge of the city. We could well have rubbed shoulders more than once in the hall's refectory line. My reminiscences elicited a warm response from the author; his signed novel remains a special possession.

Emotionally and physically, Ngugi was unhappy and uncomfortable in Leeds. He disliked the cold, the grime, the seeming lack of town planning, and the jumbly rows of buildings 'crouching like old men and women', all of which still character-ized the city in the 1960s at a time when its postmodern makeover of two decades later was only a dream. Bodington Hall offered him at least some modern design, was centrally heated, and lay close to the wild beauty of the moors. To others, myself included, the rawness of Leeds gave it a gritty charm. It was a perfect place to sup pints of Tetley's ales in straight glasses and live each day in worn jeans, long scarves, donkey jackets and army surplus greatcoats with collars turned up against the northern chill. Above all, it was one of the best places in the United Kingdom to be studying literature, as the School of English at the university had a reputa-tion for a progressive curriculum and a distinctive cadre of teachers. I can vouch for it; for instance, my weekly tutorials with the poet Geoffrey Hill at the top of an old Victorian terrace house were not to be missed. Some days I would wake in my flat fifteen minutes before the meeting, throw on my clothes, skip breakfast, and sprint up the hill to the campus so as not to be late for an experience that was invariably invigorating and often intense. Pacing the creaking boards of his office, Hill sought to instill a modicum of critical acumen in his small group of awestruck acolytes.

Intellectually, then, Ngugi benefited greatly from his time in the Leeds post-graduate programme. In the process of his own growing radicalization, he came under the influence of one of his teachers, the Marxist scholar Arnold Kettle, whose magnum opus, *An Introduction to the English Novel*, offered an alterna-tive, uncommon, and stirring method of analysing texts to that dominated by New Criticism and its Leavisite apostles. As Ngugi acknowledges, Leeds had a radical tradition that matched his own burgeoning resistance to imperialism, racism, and the class system. As the centre of the English woollen industry, Leeds saw much socialist agitation, from the Luddites through the Chartists to late-nineteenth-century local heroes such as Tom Maguire and Isabella Ford. More recently, the university was home to *Stand*, established in 1952 by Jon Silkin, later Gregory Fellow in Poetry, as a literary magazine that would 'stand' both against injustice and the forces of oppression, and for the value of literature and the arts in the waging of that struggle.

Ngugi contrasted the intellectual atmosphere there favourably with his brief experience of Oxford, where he observed fellow African students unchanged or rendered more reactionary by their experience of conservative norms and bastions of privilege. Interviewed in 1966 by fellow Leeds students, he said, 'I went to Oxford last term and some students I met there. Lord! They were worse than they ever were before coming to England', adding positively that 'invariably a "colonial" student who comes to Leeds goes back with a disturbed state of mind'. Again, I relate to Ngugi's experience. When I was interviewed for a place at Oxford, the musty college passageways suggested equally musty learning, and the porter addressed me as 'Sir' on bringing a breakfast tray to my room. These stale impressions sat uneasily with my left-wing leanings and a head full of Bob Dylan's lyrics. In an academic sense at least, arriving in Leeds was a breath of fresh air. This was Yorkshire unreconstructed; there was nothing effete, supercilious, or pretentious about the place.

Unsurprising, then, that almost everything to do with the rise of Commonwealth and especially African literature seemed bound up for a while in the School of English. In an article entitled 'Ngugi, Leeds and the establishment of African literature', James Currey, former editorial director at Heinemann, describes this relationship in detail. It was stimulated by the open-minded departmental chairmanship of A. Norman (Derry) Jeffares, eminent Irish scholar of Yeats and champion of the Commonwealth Literature movement. In 1962, Heinemann Educational Books took the intrepid step of launching its African Writers series, which was a groundbreaking list for Western readers eager to discover the best of African literature. Achebe was the founding editor. Heinemann and Leeds were soon working together through Jeffares and Keith Sambrook at the publisher. The first title in the series to appear in both paperback and hardback, in an attempt to broaden international readership, turned out to be Ngugi's *Weep Not, Child* in 1964, a text that (along with *The River Between*) Achebe had sent to the publisher with a strong recommendation.

The English department at Leeds went on to become the first in Britain to establish a chair (William Walsh in 1972) in Commonwealth literature, as the nascent study of postcolonial literature was called. Several of its younger faculty, among them Arthur Ravenscroft and Andrew Gurr, became authorities in the new field (Gurr was for a time my house warden at Bodington Hall). Leeds was also the first to hold a Commonwealth Literature conference, in 1964, out of which came the *Journal of Commonwealth Literature*, also published by Heinemann. In 1965, the scholar Eldred Durosimi Jones, from Sierra Leone, one of the most vocal proponents of integrating African literature into the African academic curriculum, took up a Commonwealth Fellowship at the university. In this respect, then, Ngugi and Leeds were a perfect fit.

As Ngugi's literary reputation continued to grow, so did his politicization. Returning to Kenya in 1968, he began a decade of writing, teaching, and agitating at the University of Nairobi. His paper 'On the abolition of the English Department', co-authored with two university colleagues and supported by Gurr, who was also there at the time, urged a change in name to the 'Department of Literature' and a revamped curriculum. Those changes, including the creation also of a department of linguistics and African languages, duly took place, and Ngugi eventually became departmental head. The paper had called for a concentric structure, 'so that African literature and related literature would constitute the inner circle with English and other European literatures in translation in the outer circles'. However, it went far beyond a local matter of campus needs, as 'it questioned the role of the organization of knowledge in the production of the colonial and postcolonial subject'. As such, it became an influential prototext in the rise of postcolonial studies.

Wali's inspirational speech at Makerere probably influenced Ngugi to renounce his English name in the 1970s. In line with tribal custom, he became Ngugi wa Thiong'o ('son of Thiong'o'). His first publication under this name, *Homecomings* (1972), a book of essays, drew partly on his postgraduate study of Caribbean writers, and tackled the question of how Kenya should move forward as an independent country as yet still shackled by the chains of neocolonialism. By the middle of the decade, Ngugi had become increasingly committed to reestablishing Gikuyu as a language of communal and creative expression. In one aspect of this effort, he involved himself with the production of Gikuyu theatre at the Kamirithu communal educational and cultural centre. Correspondingly, at the 1977 launch of his fourth novel *Petals of Blood*, he announced his intention to abandon writing in English in favour of Gikuyu, a bold yet risky move intended to subvert the dominant status of the colonialist tongue. Ngugi points out that *Petals of Blood* is 'littered with Gikuyu and Swahili words – almost as if, in the text, I was announcing the contradiction in my position and practice'. Though the book is bitter in tone, bleak in mood, and scathing in its attack on the neocolonialist bourgeoisie, the Kenyan government kept its hands off the author due to his literary stature.

That kid glove approach was not the case with a production at Kamirithu of his Gikuyu-language play *I Will Marry When I Want* (*Ngaahika Ndeenda*), co-authored with Ngugi wa Mirii, about struggling Bata shoe workers in Limuru. Less than two months after its performance Ngugi was arrested, on New Year's Eve 1977, and without trial spent the following year in solitary confinement in a maximum-security prison. A campaign by Amnesty International eventually secured his release. While incarcerated he had continued to write, on sheets of toilet paper, 'in a "room" provided free by the post-colonial state', as he wryly explains. This clandestine creativity resulted in one part of his account of imprisonment, *Detained: A Writer's Prison Diary* (1981, recently revised as *Wrestling with the Devil: A Prison Memoir*), and in a draft of *Devil on the Cross* (*Caitaani Mutharaba-ini*), one of the earliest novels written in Gikuyu, published in 1982. In that same year the authorities banned the Kamirithu centre and destroyed the theatre. Ngugi likely would have found more sympathetic company in Zimbabwe or Tanzania, where academic and literary life at the time was more open to someone of his persuasion. In the event, he may have deemed those countries still too close to home for comfort, and so he fled Kenya to begin a twenty-two-year exile first in the United Kingdom and later in the United States. Twenty years after his promising appearance at the Makerere conference, he was now a fully fledged international literary celebrity, and *faute de mieux* a political one too.

❋ ❋ ❋

Literary celebrity brings with it the prospect of being awarded major prizes for one's work. In its 118-year-old history, the Nobel Prize in Literature has been notable for its unrivalled prestige, unusual or controversial choices, occasional politicization, omission of some canonical authors, others declining the prize, and a general aura of uncertainty over how its core values and award criteria may be interpreted. In the last few years, under new chair Sara Danius, the Nobel literature committee appears to have opened up more than ever before to an oeuvre based on oral and performative elements in addition to 'purely' literary ones. This tendency, which first appeared with the award to Italian dramatist Dario Fo in 1997, manifested itself strongly in 2015 with the prize going to the Belorussian 'polyphonic' historian Svetlana Alexievich, and again in 2016 when singer-songwriter Bob Dylan was the laureate. Even the 2017 winner, British author Kazuo Ishiguro, who would seem to represent a return to a more conventional choice, reflects the committee's growing awareness of broader cultural and commercial reach via successful screen adaptations of two Ishiguro novels, *The Remains of the Day* and *Never Let Me Go*. Yet both Dylan and Ishiguro seemed faintly embarrassed to receive the prize. Others have felt it marks the beginning of the end; Samuel Beckett, the 1969 laureate, infamously described winning it as a disaster. Nonetheless, love it or hate it, the Nobel remains the world's foremost literary prize and the one that perennially garners most public attention. And for all its hints of a growing populism, equally it has been awarded sometimes to unheralded authors and countries whose literature is less visible internationally. Moreover, as Alex Shephard writes in a 2017 *New Republic* article, 'it remains the most powerful tool in upsetting the hegemony of corporate publishing, which has created a homogeneous book culture driven by sales and popularity'.

For the last fifteen years or so, Ngugi has been repeatedly tipped to win the prize, though the committee has chosen a black African writer only once, Wole Soyinka in 1986, and overlooked the claims of his fellow Nigerian, Chinua Achebe. Only five other African writers have won the prize, four of whom are white (J. M. Coetzee, Nadine Gordimer, Doris Lessing, and Albert Camus, who anyway would first be considered French) and one is Arab, Naguib Mahfouz. And those laureates whom, like Ngugi, we consider to be postcolonial authors number but three: Soyinka, V. S. Naipaul, and Derek Walcott.

The criteria for the awarding of the prize, initially strong on humanitarian and idealistic qualities according to Alfred Nobel's original conception, have evolved necessarily into a more pragmatic set of requirements that seek to guard the essence of that conception and may be encapsulated in the continued use of several of Nobel's own words: 'outstanding work in an ideal direction'. Though this phrase remains as open to question as previous ones, it suggests that primary literary quality should be bolstered by evidence of a moral conscience and lofty principles of thought.

It would seem, then, that Ngugi checks all the boxes. His lengthy career has earned him a global reputation for creating a substantial body of imaginative and uncompromising texts, often against considerable personal odds. In addition to his short stories, novels, plays, and memoirs (the latter having now reached three volumes appearing from 2010 to 2016), we may recognize a powerful and influential body of criticism and theory that has been instrumental in the quest to develop both post-colonial studies and African cultural independence. Beginning back in 1968 with 'On the abolition of the English Department', these texts later include *Decolonizing the Mind: The Politics of Language in African Literature* (1986), in which he exposed the collusion of former colonial powers and their neocolonialist successors in a hegemonic shift from cannon to canon; *Moving the Centre: The Struggle for Cultural Freedoms* (1993), in which he argued for seismic shifts of both intranational and international power and influence; *Penpoints, Gunpoints, and Dreams* (1996), in which he located the nexus of power relations in the 'temporal and spatial organization of knowledge'; and *Globalectics: Theory and the Politics of Knowing* (2012), in which he went beyond his earlier Africanist position to argue for the 'liberation of literature from the strait-jackets of nationalism', and to locate the postcolonial in a Blakean vision of fair exchange, of a balance of 'hereness and thereness' within world literature and among world languages. Thus, as his own thought has evolved, he has been able also to reach a compromise with those who had criticized his earlier avowal of abrogation as simply reproducing the absolutist structural models of the colonialism it had purported to displace. And though Ngugi's creative writing, notwithstanding the magical realist elements of his comic novel *Wizard of the Crow* (2006), does not suggest the late flowering of a hybridist newly engaged in creative appropriation, he has gradually moved his own theoretical centre closer to more sophisticated notions of postcolonial textuality.

Ngugi is a literary celebrity because of the international renown of his works and what lies behind them, namely a sustained commitment to the freedom and rights of oppressed, subjugated, and underprivileged people, not only on the African continent or in his native land but wherever such struggles are deemed to be justified. He has paid a high price for his commitment in the form of imprisonment and exile. In 2004, after Kenyan dictator Daniel arap Moi had been out of power for two years, Ngugi returned to Nairobi only for him and his wife Njeeri to be robbed and physically assaulted by a gang of armed men. More recently, though, he has enjoyed a guarded rapprochement with the Kenyan government under its current president, Uhuru Kenyatta.

Why, then, has Ngugi not won the Nobel? Could it be on account of a life of political activism underpinned by a consistent attack on Western imperialism? Hardly, since the Nobel committee has rarely shown bias against liberal anti-establishment figures. Nonetheless, in 1989, when Salman Rushdie was widely tipped to win, two committee members publicly resigned over their belief that Rushdie's alleged blasphemy of Islam in his novel *The Satanic Verses* might lead to a lack of overall support for his candidacy. Then again, Soyinka won despite also having been imprisoned and exiled. In 1958, the committee chose Boris Pasternak, though the author felt obliged to decline the prize under Soviet pressure. And in 1964 it chose Jean-Paul Sartre, though he too declined it in protest at its reactionary status.

Ngugi's rejection of Eurocentrism and later of literary nationalism as well as his refusal to kowtow to Western literary norms might be viewed as having counted against him. Might he have excluded himself from serious consideration by opting for an exceptionally minor language, one that lies beyond even the comprehension of 80 per cent of his fellow Kenyans? We should remember that he made his name internationally by writing in English, and has continued to make his work widely accessible in translation by his own hand or another's. We cannot view him therefore as having summarily rejected Western culture and its literary system. And if we note the Nobel committee's openness to the performativity of Fo, Alexievich, and Dylan, we cannot see Ngugi's defense of the value of orature in literature, an integral part of his globalectic theory, as having worked against him in any way.

A provocative argument against Ngugi winning the Nobel appeared in a 2010 *New York Times* article, 'In Africa, the Laureate's curse', by Nigerian author and journalist Adaobi Tricia Nwaubani. In that year, Ngugi again had been a favourite to win, but the prize eventually went to the Peruvian novelist Mario Vargas Llosa. Nwaubani argued that a Nobel for Ngugi, at least for then, would not serve African literary interests, as it would perpetuate aspirations on the part of younger writers to become the 'next Ngugi' by writing polished and imitative texts at the expense of more individualistic or idiosyncratic ones. For Nwaubani, even to be nominated for the prize would represent appropriation by a dominant Western literary establishment. Such an embrace would thus prove counterproductive to the goals of an independent and progressive African literature. At the core of her argument is a call for the establishment of African prizes to celebrate African writers. Only then might those writers be encouraged to express themselves in original forms and styles.

To a great extent, however, Nwaubani plays devil's advocate. She hints that she would like Ngugi to win anyhow, and her argument seeks rather to emphasize a basic problem in the quest for postcolonial cultural autonomy. By opposing a proliferation of literary texts in tribal languages, she recognizes that although it has worked for Ngugi as an already established author, it would serve only to obscure the talents of younger writers and hinder their emergence onto to a wider stage. 'We suffer enough from tribal differences already', she adds, while further noting that African-language publishing, chronically short of funds and resources, is a struggling industry, with publishers largely unwilling to invest in untested or innovative writing. Whether disingenuously or not, Nwaubani argues that a Nobel to Ngugi would perpetuate a certain type of African postcolonial writing which in her view has become safe and predictable in the eyes of the literary world at large. Yet again, we may counter that such an accolade could refocus those eyes in a timely manner on African literature in both indigenous and European languages.

Even so, we should not allow the prestige of the Nobel to blind us to its inherent limitations. Those limitations were placed in stark perspective in 2018 with the decision not to award the literature prize in that year due to a sexual scandal involving the husband of one of the members of the Swedish Academy, the body responsible for choosing the laureate. The scandal served to reinforce internal and external accusations of sexism, secretiveness, leaks, and financial malpractice. Consequently, in the cloak-and-dagger atmosphere surrounding this group of eighteen members elected for life, we may wonder if any author would truly wish to be its chosen one.

Furthermore, I recap a phrase I used early on: the 'purely' literary. For what may that possibly mean? The Nobel, no less than any other major literary prize, has always faced the tricky question of how outstanding literary quality may be determined. After all, critical opinion is never innocent or absolute, and attributions of quality are ultimately subjective notions. It seems anyway that winning the prize may not be particularly significant to Ngugi, since the dynamics of his globalectic vision would appear to relegate the Nobel to the status of one qualitative element among many in a decentred literary world system. Perhaps this may account for Ngugi's relaxed attitude, neither indifferent nor invested, to his chance of winning the prize. As he told a recent interviewer, to win would be 'validating but not essential', which is perhaps how we may come more generally to view this prize of prizes as the literature of the twenty-first century evolves.

7

Roaring through life: John Seymour

The celebrity status of John Seymour is not primarily literary but rather ecological, as a guru of the back-to-earth movement in the United Kingdom whose primer in that field, *The Complete Book of Self-Sufficiency* (1976), has sold over a million copies in thirty countries. Though he had long formulated his basic creed of localized, small-scale, simple living, and with his wife Sally had published on self-sufficiency as early as 1961 in *The Fat of The Land*, Seymour – like Scott and Helen Nearing in North America, whose *Living the Good Life* had appeared in 1954 – influenced the rise and rode the wave of environmental consciousness which crested in the 1970s in a largely rural communalism emerging from the alternative society of the late 1960s. This was the time when zeitgeist books such as E. F. Schumacher's *Small is Beautiful* (1973) and Frances Moore Lappé's *Diet for a Small Planet* (1971) offered, like Seymour's, both a philosophy of and a hands-on guide to alternative, eco-friendly lifestyles. And in the United Kingdom, this subculture found a popular mainstream expression in the BBC television comedy series, *The Good Life* (1975).

Seymour wrote extensively, putting his name to forty-one books, most of which are single-authored. Given such a constant output, averaging two books a year, their quality is inevitably uneven, but at his best Seymour is an eloquent and persuasive writer. He commands a vernacular prose style underpinned by an exceptional knowledge of a range of subjects. Yet he wears his learning lightly. Above all, he knows how to tell a good story. Seymour the gifted raconteur, the keen interlocutor, transfers well to his written page, so that one feels genuinely welcomed into his company. He enhances his informal style by a lively, occasionally self-deprecating sense of humour. Equally he can reveal his ornery side, especially when invoking any one of his familiar *bêtes noires*, such as big business, road and air traffic, environmental pollution, and heedless urbanization. We meet a man of strong tastes and opinions, but one who strives to be fair in argument and open to the views of others.

Seymour's control of narrative structure works best in his characteristic non-fictional mode. In his travel-based memoirs, for instance, he opts frequently for a 'then and now' perspective which allows him to draw positive or negative conclusions from his observations. Nonetheless, he tried his hand at fiction in an apocalyptic novel, *Retrieved from the Future* (1996), about an ungovernable Britain, but appeared less sure of himself when faced with the demands of characterization and plotting than when recounting his own experiences within the largely episodic structure of his memoirs. Even a practical manual of self-sufficiency like *The Fat of the Land* works as a memoir. His personal tone takes the reader into his confidence, so he is

John Seymour

able to air his ideas and opinions of past and present, of history and society, without being programmatic or seeming detached.

Seymour has a great eye for detail. His daughter Anne confirms that he possessed an uncommonly sharp memory throughout his life, and put it to good use in his writing. Though he kept notebooks especially for his earlier travel books, his power of recall allowed him to write with unerring accuracy about his experiences. Though he exaggerates occasionally in order to make a point, Seymour is not a writer who takes poetic license. Anyway, he would not have needed to, as his travels around the world proved sufficient to his literary goals. Above all, he stands out both as a fierce critic of progress for its own sake and as an individualist who values diverse cultures as well as the small but meaningful distinctions among people and places. Whenever he sets a scene, it cannot be complete in his mind without those who populate the landscape, and he delights in introducing his reader to a rich gallery of often eccentric and outspoken persons whose stories match his own in being by turns comical, salutary, and wise.

I first encountered John Seymour's writing in the form of a birthday gift from my grandmother in 1971. It was *The Companion Guide to East Anglia*, published in the previous year as part of a series by the British publisher Collins with the stated aim of providing 'a Companion, in the person of the author, who knows intimately the places and people of whom he writes, and is able to communicate this knowledge and affection to his readers'. It took little time for me to realize that Seymour fitted that authorial bill perfectly. He proves to be a true companion, ever ready, as if on the reader's shoulder, to share with wit and panache his wealth of geographical, historical, and social knowledge. He is alive to architectural features and qualities of landscape, as any good guide-book writer should be, but there is so much more residing in the spirit and verve of the book. Both to practical purpose and out of sheer human interest, he enjoys introducing the regional visitor to all manner of interesting places and persons he may come across on the way. In turn, the ideal travellers – his readers – should have, like the author, a breezy outlook and a scant respect for mass thinking and conventional behaviour. They should also enjoy being regaled with a host of anecdotes, at the telling of which the author excels. Perhaps the highest praise I can give the volume is that I always open its pages excited to discover yet another quirky historical detail or unusual human being. I like too to imagine that W. G. Sebald, in writing *The Rings of Saturn* (1998), another genre-bending gem of East Anglian nonfiction, in his case based on the author's walking tour of Suffolk, may have been inspired by Seymour's eye for the unusual, by his adventurous spirit, and by his iconoclastic views, for instance on the destruction of the natural environment.

Seymour went on to write three more books in the series during the next five years, on the coasts of South-West, North-East, and South-East England – all perfect topics for a writer who was a keen sailor and at home as much on water as on land. No surprise, then, that the first chapter of his East Anglian guide begins with the sentence: 'Ideally Woodbridge should be approached from the sea, as the first East Anglians approached it, up the beautiful Deben estuary.' As for the old publishing house of William Collins, Sons, founded in Edinburgh in 1819, it was swallowed up by corporatism, though its name survives in Harper Collins, the British subsidiary of the huge American conglomerate Harper & Row. Seymour, who fiercely opposed all big business interests, would doubtless have been unimpressed by this fate.

I discovered later that Seymour had been writing more or less in this manner from the beginning of his literary career. In 1934, aged 20, he left Britain for Africa, and returned after the Second World War, during which he did military service on that continent. Following his first five years in South Africa, he joined the King's African Rifles at the outbreak of war and fought in Ethiopia (later in Ceylon and Burma). He returned to Africa in 1954. The account of his earlier visit forms the basis of *One Man's Africa* (1956), his fourth book, the first having also been a travel memoir, *The Hard Way to India* (1951).

He divides his African narrative into two equal parts of 'Down south' and 'Up north', soon confirming his experiences in both halves as pivotal in his adopting a set of liberal, humanitarian principles and values, ones that became a cornerstone of his lifelong vision of a better world. Africa allowed him to get back to basics. He admires all that runs counter to the 'deadening, all-conquering Western way of life

... of cloying respectability, deadly mediocrity, efficiency for the sake of efficiency, machines for making more machines'. He is already beginning to draw the blueprint for a self-sufficient alternative lifestyle, as shown, for instance, in his appreciation of the simple, organic hunter-gatherer life of the South African Bushmen, one of whom, a man named Joseph, takes Seymour hunting for lions and impresses him greatly with his independence, intelligence, and resourcefulness.

At the same time, Seymour was developing a literary style that would serve him well in almost everything he wrote thereafter. He established a standard pattern for his writing in his early work. Whether recounting lion hunting on the veld, snoek catching in the South Atlantic, doing shifts in the copper mines of Northern Rhodesia, or engaging in sorties against Mussolini's army in Ethiopia, his energetic prose matches his young man's story. He combines detailed descriptions with a narrative thrust, bringing to life a curious cast of characters, both native and European, with a correspondingly deft use of dialogue. Seymour belongs to the tail end of a generation of footloose young British adventurer-writers that included such figures as Graham Greene, T. E. Lawrence, and Patrick Leigh Fermor. Despite the vigourous physicality of his African life, there is also evidence of the literary incli-nation that would begin to bear fruit in his forties. For example, within the space of a single paragraph describing his work in Rhodesia, he twice invokes the canon of English literature, suggesting he may be 'the first man to have read all of George Bernard Shaw's plays in the sump of a copper mine', and then evoking further his subterranean surroundings with the famous images of 'caverns measureless to man' and 'sunless sea' from Samuel Taylor Coleridge's 'Kubla Khan'.

It is remarkable that Seymour, despite his own privileged English upbringing, sided very early with the native Africans, whom he perceived as ever disadvantaged by a blatantly unjust system of land ownership and power relations instituted and perpetuated by imperial and colonial rule. Furthermore, he soon understood how that racist system generated and maintained a vicious cycle of social and economic subservience, one which manifested itself worst in the utterly degraded life of the urbanized native, for instance in the dreadful shanty-towns of greater Johannesburg. He adds that life is little better for the itinerant farm worker who, despite his rural existence, is 'looked upon by the law not as a man, but as a unit of labour' and is therefore 'a prisoner in his own country'. Regarding other of my essays in this collec-tion, I imagine Seymour would have found himself agreeing much more with Ngugi wa Thiong'o than with Karen Blixen, especially when he writes, for instance, of black South African farm workers whose 'sole *raison d'être* was to work for, and wait on, the White Man …. They could have no land of their own, no community, no country, no traditions, no intercourse with others of their race, and no freedom.' Seymour opposed Europeans farming in Africa, if an indigenous farming community existed, and he firmly believed that given the right opportunities for small-scale cultivation native farmers would grow better crops. Nonetheless, while acknowledging that he has 'criticized strongly some of the actions and ideas of some of the white people who live in Africa', he grants that he understands and can sympathize with their outlook. For Seymour, as a *kaffirboetjie* (or 'pro-native') as he was often called good-naturedly by his Afrikaner friends, the human quality of individuals of whichever background always outweighs the shortcomings of the society to which they belong.

Seymour paints a rich and detailed picture of pre-war African life. Sometimes this detail becomes highly technical, as in his section on the Rhodesian mining industry. He appears so interested throughout his book in sharing his extensive knowledge of the minutiae of production processes within hunter-gathering, agricultural, fishing, or industrial milieus that he occasionally risks diverting the reader from the forward movement of his narrative. But this is a minor quibble. His memoir effectively introduces his soon-to-become familiar 'then and now' technique by recognizing the winds of change rising in Africa at the time of his return there in the early 1950s.

Part memoir of his life as a smallholder in Suffolk in the late-1950s, part handbook on sustainable living, *The Fat of the Land* established Seymour as a British ecological freethinker at a time when the call for self-sufficiency was still a faint one. As Britain finally shrugged off the shackles of postwar austerity, a growing prosperity stimulated consumerism and materialistic values in British society. Seymour's contrary views were already well developed, and he saw early what he firmly believed to be the writing on the wall. Most of what made *The Complete Book of Self-Sufficiency* such a milestone fifteen years later is contained in preliminary form in this earthy, humorous book enhanced by Sally Seymour's illustrations.

After Seymour married Sally in 1954, the couple pursued a semi-nomadic lifestyle which he had already been supporting by writing travel books and scripting for the BBC. He was under no illusion about his incentive to write, calling himself a 'word monger', serving up words 'in whatever form I could get paid for them'. On acquiring The Broom, a smallholding built around two vacant farm cottages near the Suffolk coast, the couple took out a twenty-five-year lease at an annual rent of £25 plus rates, a modest outlay even for that relatively inexpensive decade.

Their move struck a chord with me, as I was familiar with inexpensive East Anglian residency, a possibility that remained open to the end of the 1970s. In 1971, as a postgraduate student seeking rural isolation to write a dissertation, I rented a disused cottage on Wong Farm in Great Melton, Norfolk, on a gentleman's agreement at a rate of £12 a month, a nominal figure that matched my meagre income from a student grant. The cottage, which required only some redecoration, was suitably remote despite its location fairly close to Norwich. And with fewer farmworkers in employment, and those who remained tending to prefer their own home to a tied one, the farmer was glad to have someone willing to occupy the place. Its curious Chinese-sounding name derived rather from an old Germanic word (*vang*) for a field. The property boom of the 1980s definitively ended these opportunities; such wild, wonderful, and cheap accommodation would be all but impossible to find today.

John and Sally Seymour had no car and few material goods but many tools and implements, and they were fully self-supporting for their food. Despite others perceiving them as leading an eccentric and deprived way of life, Seymour gleefully declares that they are 'rip-roaring cranks' having a great deal of fun. Equally wryly, he observes that Henry David Thoreau got away with having precious little apparatus at Walden by being willing to live 'almost exclusively on beans'. Besides, when he fancied a good dinner, Thoreau had only to take a short walk into Concord to resume a seat at his mother's table. Viewing the produce trade as 'a world of thieves and rogues and bounders', and inspired to do otherwise by William Cobbett's *Cottage Economy* (1821), Seymour finds himself almost inevitably drawn into a 'peasant' system as opposed to the 'industrial' one holding sway beyond the limits of his home. Nor is he under any illusions about his ideal of mixed farming ('a big variety of crops and stock') being contrary to the '*spiritus mundi*' of specialization advocated by government, agribusiness, and the farming press. He acknowledges his 'anachronistic' lifestyle as a paradoxical form of progress based on *re*gress, *re*vival, and *re*cuperation.

The 1974 edition includes a final chapter, 'Thirteen years after', in which Seymour, by then resettled in a 'still peasant' sector of Welsh society, reflects that the vision of fully cooperative American-style agrarian-communitarian experiments is impossible in the United Kingdom because of both the price of land and the planning laws. Finally, he counters charges of selfishness by stating his own eighteen-year record of happily escapist independence and by asserting that nobody *has* to be a self-supporter, but that anybody should be free to be one 'if he can show first that he knows how to do it'.

By the time of *I'm a Stranger Here Myself* (1978), a memoir of life on his Pembrokeshire farm and the true sequel to *The Fat of the Land*, Seymour was both an ecological celebrity and, on the strength of *The Complete Book of Self-Sufficiency*, a literary one too. Subsequently he moved to Ireland, where he spent most of his remaining life, only returning to the family-owned farm in Wales during his latter days. In 1988 he published *England Revisited: A Countryman's Nostalgic Journey*, another blend of memoir and travel book written in his characteristic style. It recounts the trips he made, on these occasions with his partner Angela Ashe, back to six familiar areas of England – the Yorkshire Dales, the Northumberland coast, the Welsh Marches, North Devon, the South Devon and Dorset border, and East Anglia, the latter marking pilgrimages to his childhood home in Essex and to the smallholding in Suffolk where his commitment to self-sufficient living had found its earliest expression.

Using his 'then and now' perspective again to good effect, he registers a strong objection to a new 'Age of Waste', in which valuable natural resources continue to be squandered. He sees this happening, for instance, in the mass planting of a single species of tree, in which 'the necessary trimmings from plantation trees are left on the ground', unlike the old forestry method of mixed planting whereby multiple reuses of different types of timber occurred. Yet, by the late 1980s, he was acknowledging that Seymour's First Law ('All change is for the worst') was no longer a constant to his mind, and that British society was finally learning some valuable lessons in the arts of conservation, restoration, and environmental management. In these respects, the 1950s through the 1970s had been largely bleak decades; now there was growing room for optimism. As he revisited these areas, mainly on foot, he was pleasantly surprised to observe various constructive initiatives that indicated a change for the better; for instance, in the regeneration of canals for the leisure industry. As he points out, on walking a towpath at Ellesmere in Shropshire, '50 years ago you would not have believed that one mile of narrow canal would have survived in England for a decade: such was the ferocity of the so-called British Waterways Board in its effort to destroy the entire system.'

Unfortunately, such positive turns at local levels had not extended to the national level, at which during the 1980s multinational corporatism, right-wing politics, and naked greed thrived in the era of Thatcherism and in its assault on the traditional British social fabric. Seymour leaves us in no doubt that he still wholeheartedly detests and resists this free market ideology and its values.

He shows his adeptness in moving from specific descriptions to general observations, as in a passage describing his horror at getting stuck on a bicycle amid a tangle of busy roads and bridges outside Exeter. This ghastly experience prompts him to conclude that he is unable to 'believe that this frenetic rushing about really helps people to achieve a better understanding of themselves or of the Universe or gets them, in any way, nearer to God. It merely distracts them, stops them from thinking or feeling, gives them an illusion of business and power and, if they do enough of it, gives them gastric ulcers.' It might seem easy to view Seymour as a hidebound traditionalist, as an old fogey whose nostalgia and preference for traditional ways of life prevents him from embracing progress. I believe the passage quoted above indicates the exact opposite to be the case. Seymour was a deeply radical thinker in the sense that he refused a blind faith in modernity, remaining sceptical of many of its claims and promises, and viewing much of it as a dehumanizing and deeply divisive force.

It may seem surprising that Seymour defends field sports, but he does so only in the interest of wildlife conservation for, as a staunch opponent of agribusiness, he argues that land kept for different forms of hunting has 'helped to prevent the whole country from becoming one huge barley and wheat prairie'. Yet his distaste for widespread land ownership remains as strong as ever, whether it is land held by the gentry, by wealthy businesspeople, or by farmers seduced by big food producers into ploughing and clearing every available inch of their acreage in search of additional profits. He cites this latter phenomenon to be a main reason why he forsook East Anglia for Wales and then Ireland.

Ireland is the subject of his 1992 memoir, *Blessed Isle: One Man's Ireland*. This book is the story of an Englishman's unconditional love of another country. Seymour's first visits to the country were in the late 1950s and early 1960s, so his tried and tested comparative perspective works well again here, as he returns in the company of Angela Ashe whom he had earlier 'adopted' unofficially on his farm in Wales and with whom in 1978 he settled on a farm at Killowen in County Wexford.

As clear minded as ever about the rights of native people to their land, Seymour does not flinch from criticism of colonial English oppression of Ireland from the sixteenth to the twentieth centuries. At pains to state that he will always side with the small nation or ethnic group against the bully, he believes that England and later Great Britain should have left Ireland alone. He reserves his greatest opprobrium for the British having 'acted in the worst tradition of rapacious landownership', a tradition that allowed an Anglo-Irish ruling class to build 'enormous and sumptuous' mansions such as those he sees dotting the landscape – for instance, Fota House near Cork – while the native people, reduced to utter dependency, were faced with eviction and starvation. A man of architectural taste and historical sensitivity, he can admire the beauty of those country houses, but cannot 'rejoice that they were built for they were founded on injustice'.

It is a happy and moving memoir, notwithstanding his tone of regret and indignation over the tragic history of Ireland. And, as we have come to expect of Seymour, there is no shortage of humorous encounters with eccentric personalities, such as the unnamed reclusive tailor in County Kerry, who made suits for Shaw, and hoards a collection of postcards from the great man, of whose identity he remains blissfully unaware. Seymour is ever willing to send himself up too, as when, on visiting the 1838 Protestant Asylum in Youghal, 'an almshouse for decayed soldiers', he was 'tempted to bang on the door to see if they would take me in since I answer to that description'. Decayed or not, with characteristic energy and determination, he keeps right on to the end of the road, in this instance bringing him to the Atlantic shore of County Donegal where he gazes out to sea in the hope of sighting the legendary *Hy-Brasail*, or Blessed Isle, a vision that appears every seven years. And then he thinks that perhaps he is already there.

Seymour was such a prolific author that some of his later books understandably tend to repeat less successfully the formula he had come up with early in his career: a combination of travel writing, memoir, and a gospel of self-sufficiency, with elements of all three often contained within a single volume. Nonetheless, his disdain for the false values of the 'progressive' modern world – for its voracious encroachments and infernal machines, most notably the dreaded 'horseless carriage' and airplane – never wavers, though as an inveterate wanderer he appreciates the convenience of credit cards. Nor does his enthusiasm flag for the simple pleasures of eating, drinking, singing, dancing, and interacting convivially with other human beings. His son-in-law David puts it simply: he 'roared through life'. Those joys, allied to his philosophy of sustainable living, remained for him the keys to a less complicated and more fulfilling time on earth.

8

Butterfly and tiger:
Octavio Paz and Rosario Castellanos

In the classical Chinese dynasties, it was unthinkable for a person holding high political office not to be an accomplished poet. The establishment of a mandarinate through the civil service examination guaranteed this administration of the empire by aesthetes for centuries to come. On an even higher level of power, the unhinged, bloodthirsty Sui emperor Yang Kuang was nonetheless a masterful versifier who waxed lyrical about late spring. This idea of literati as politicians and rulers, comparable to Plato's theory of the philosopher-king, recurs in the lives of many towering literary figures such as Cicero, Niccolò Machiavelli, Thomas More, and John Milton, whom Oliver Cromwell rewarded for his Parliamentarian allegiance with the exotic title of secretary for foreign tongues. Later, as the nineteenth century beckoned, Matthew Lewis was so bored by life in The Hague as a British attaché to the Netherlands that he found a way to excite himself and others by hurriedly composing *The Monk*. This dual occupation happens in music too: Giuseppe Verdi, an ardent supporter of Count Cavour and of the *risorgimento*, became a member of the Italian parliament for four years following his country's independence in 1861.

In the United States and the United Kingdom, the author as statesman grows rare after Benjamin Franklin and Thomas Jefferson in the former, and Benjamin Disraeli in the latter. Thereafter, in Anglo-American culture and that of other nations where the protestant work ethic reigns supreme, artists and intellectuals generally come to be viewed as unsuited to or uninterested in the holding of prominent political office, their literary activity deemed to be either a socio-economic luxury irrelevant to the pragmatic and formal business of governing a country or a private calling altogether above it. In the United States, the artist turned politician has occasionally re-emerged, but he comes now from the ranks of mass entertainers such as the movie stars Ronald Reagan, Arnold Schwarzenegger, and Clint Eastwood. We rarely hear of writers, painters, or composers assuming major public office. The great twentieth-century British exception is Winston S. Churchill, winner of the 1953 Nobel Prize in Literature, who was an author of fiction, albeit of limited repute, before he gained political fame. Nonetheless, he would never have won his Nobel had he not first become a great statesman and orator, who parlayed his experience into a series of monumental biographical and historical works.

Elsewhere, this overlooking of writers is less common. We may consider Léopold

Sédar Senghor and Václav Havel, for instance, as having become presidents of the Senegalese and Czech republics respectively. In France, André Malraux became the nation's first minister of culture under Charles de Gaulle.

In Latin America especially, the influence of the intellectual elite (*pensadores*) on public life has long rendered it customary for leading artists and writers to hold senior governmental, ambassadorial, or civil service positions. In Nicaragua, for instance, under the Sandinistas, it seemed for a while as if everybody in government was a writer. President Daniel Ortega wrote poetry in prison from 1967 to 1974, while Sergio Ramírez, his vice-president from 1985 to 1990, and Ernesto Cardenal, his minister of culture from 1979 to 1987, are both prominent poets.

According to Rachel Popma, a translator of Rosario Castellanos's poetry, 'in Latin America ... it is often felt that there is no better representative of one's country and culture than one who moves and shapes that culture through his/her art'. In modern Mexican literature, Castellanos and Octavio Paz spring immediately to mind as having followed this dual career. Celebrated as writers first and foremost (Castellanos much later than Paz, having become internationally visible as a major feminist author mainly through the critical work of Maureen Ahern in the 1980s), neither author held high political office, but both consistently involved themselves in Mexican political life. Paz in particular achieved a measure of notoriety as a result of his contentious contributions to various ideological debates. Both doubtless would have agreed with Jamaican author Olive Senior's view that 'we are all enmeshed in politics because we are all citizens of somewhere ... and we cannot escape being shaped by political decisions, big and small'.

Along with Chile's Pablo Neruda, Paz's stature as Latin America's leading twentieth-century poet is uncontested, and was confirmed by the award of the literary Nobel in 1990, eight years before his death. Born in Mexico City in 1914, he published his first collection of poems in 1933. By the 1960s, his poetic talent had matured into a daring formal and technical command of language that blended his nativized surrealism with a deep interest in Marxism, mythology, Oriental philosophy, and especially pre-Columbian civilization. He had become a truly visionary poet. His masterpiece remains *Sun-stone* (*Piedra de sol*, 1963), a complex expression of myth, history, and philosophical ideas, whose title refers to the engraved stone calendar of the Aztecs.

Though always primarily a poet, Paz believed in a necessary symbiosis of art and politics. Having fought in the Spanish Civil War, he eagerly entered the Mexican political arena as a commentator before starting a diplomatic career. In 1946 he was posted as a cultural attaché to France, where he revelled in the vibrant postwar Parisian literary and philosophical scenes. In 1962 he took up the post of ambassador to India, though he was reassigned promptly to Japan. In 1968 he resigned his post in protest at his government's massacre of students in Tlatelolco during the 1968 Mexico Olympic Games. His decision was in complete accord with his belief that, however dedicated to his art (and for Paz poetry was akin to a religious faith) a poet has civic and moral responsibilities, and that poetic practice and political action must at some point merge. In *Poetry, Myth, Revolution* (1989), writing in the spirit of Shelley, he declared that 'the defense of poetry, scorned in our century, [is] inseparable from the defense of freedom'.

His tireless search for a perfect rhetoric of opposites, inculcated in him by the dynamics of surrealist juxtaposition and Marxist dialectic, led him to argue, as in his 1982 Neustadt International Prize for Literature acceptance speech, that 'Plurality is Universality, and Universality is the acknowledging of the admirable diversity of man and his works'. Furthermore, in *The Other Voice: Essays on Modern Poetry* (1990), Paz attacks postmodernism and consumerism. His refusal to accept political fashion or dogma caused him, a model liberal democrat of a broad leftist persuasion, to clash with those on the far side of revolutionary thinking. In *Vuelta*, the literary-political review he founded in 1976, he opposed extremism of any kind, whether it was communism, guerilla violence, or Latin American military dictatorships. Consequently, in the 1980s, his withering criticism of the Sandinista rebels in Nicaragua saw him branded unfairly as an apologist for the right and for US imperialism: '*Reagan rapaz, tu amigo es Octavio Paz*', as one chant went.

Also born in Mexico City, in 1925, Rosario Castellanos came from a wealthy landowning family descended from Spanish conquistadors. From an early age, Castellanos grew up on the family lands in Comitán in the south-eastern state of Chiapas, which borders Guatemala and the Pacific coast, and where early Mayan ruins exist in the jungle region. In many ways more Guatemalan than Mexican, the state is home to the native Chamula Indians, and was the source in the 1980s of the Zapatista rebel army which in 1994 declared continuing open war on the central government. As a child, Castellanos received scant attention from her parents, who made it painfully clear that she was less important to them than her younger brother Benjamin, even more so after his untimely death when she was still very young. Experiencing thus a solitary childhood, she sought refuge in literature, though her parents deemed its pursuit unsuitable for their daughter. Her literary enthusiasm could not be dampened, however, and her privileged social status at least allowed her to witness early in life the sharp racial and cultural divisions in Mexican society, and from her superior position to observe uneasily the life of the native people. She would imbue much of her subsequent fiction and poetry with this precocious knowledge and understanding.

During her girlhood, Mexican President Lázaro Cárdenas introduced a governmental reform scheme that stripped the upper class of most of their landed possessions. It was a blessing in disguise for Castellanos, who otherwise might have found herself tied rigidly to a conventional female role in Chiapan society. In a 1970 essay, 'Man of destiny', she expresses her admiration of and gratitude to Cárdenas for ending her family's privileged way of life and thus freeing her to choose for herself. The family moved back to Mexico City after losing its *hacienda* in 1941, though Castellanos later returned to do official cultural work in Chiapas, partly out of a sense of debt to those native people who had been cast in servile roles. While studying at university in Mexico City, she involved herself with a group of writers known as 'the Eight' and later as the 'Generation of 1950', but it was not until her parents both died in 1948 that she, sole heir to the family fortune, felt completely free of social expectations and proceeded to adopt literature as her profession. Her earliest publications were poetry; almost a decade later she began to publish fiction. Her reputation grew steadily through the 1950s and 1960s.

The ideological content of much of her writing made it no surprise that from 1967 she, like Paz, set out to forge a parallel political career in which, again like Paz, she strove to keep a personal and intellectual distance from establishment life and its conformist values. After having done her share of cultural service to the Mexican nation and to the state of Chiapas, President Luis Echeverría named her ambassador to Israel in 1971. Tragically, her twin careers were cut short in August 1974 when she was accidentally electrocuted at home in Tel Aviv.

After 300 years of Spanish rule up to 1821 and less than a century of independence, modern Mexico dates essentially from the 1910 Revolution, which broke the old neocolonial landowning system which had kept 96 per cent of the national population as landless peasants, with the other 4 per cent owning the large estates known as *haciendas* and the smallholdings known as *ranchos*. The economic and social reforms that gathered pace from the 1920s went along with a huge population increase and with a redefinition of Mexican identity. It is against this backdrop that modern Mexican literature emerged, a literature free to ask questions of and to recover some of the history of this ancient land that had been home to numerous pre-Columbian civilizations, notably the Maya, the Toltec, and the Aztec. Paz and Castellanos pose these questions and seek to recover this history powerfully in their writing, two notable examples being Paz's poem 'Obsidian butterfly' (*Mariposa obsidiana*) and Castellanos's short story 'Death of the tiger' (*La muerte del tigre*).

'Obsidian butterfly' comes from a 1951 collection of prose poems, the first of its kind in Spanish and entitled *Eagle or Sun?* (*Aguila o Sol?*), which in Spanish also means 'heads or tails?' A key passage for understanding the context of 'Obsidian butterfly' is in *The Labyrinth of Solitude* (1950), Paz's celebrated exploration of the body and soul of Mexico. Paz writes:

> It is no secret to anyone that Mexican Catholicism is centered about the cult of the Virgin of Guadalupe. In the first place, she is an Indian Virgin; in the second place, the scene of her appearance to the Indian Juan Diego was a hill

Octavio Paz, Malmo Poetry Festival, 1988

that formerly contained a sanctuary dedicated to Tonantzin, 'Our Mother', the Aztec goddess of fertility. We know that the Conquest coincided with the apogee of the cult of two masculine divinities: Quetzalcóatl, the self-sacrificing god, and Huitzilopochtli, the young warrior-god. The defeat of these gods – which is what the Conquest meant to the Indian world because it was the end of a cosmic cycle and the inauguration of a new divine kingdom – caused the faithful to return to the ancient feminine deities. This phenomenon of a return to the maternal womb, so well-known to the psychologist, is without doubt one of the determining causes of the swift popularity of the cult of the Virgin. The Indian goddesses were goddesses of fecundity, linked to the cosmic rhythms, the vegetative processes and agrarian rites. The Catholic Virgin is also the mother (some Indian pilgrims still call her Guadalupe-Tonantzin), but her principal attribute is not to watch over the fertility of the earth but to provide refuge for the unfortunate. The situation has changed: the worshippers do not try to make sure of their harvests but to find a mother's lap. The Virgin is the consolation of the poor, the shield of the weak, the help of the oppressed. In sum, she is the Mother of orphans.

'Obsidian butterfly' is narrated from the point of view of Itzpapálotl, a goddess sometimes confused with the maternal goddesses. All of these female divinities that replaced the defeated gods were fused from the sixteenth century onward into the Christian cult of the Virgin of Guadalupe. Itzpapálotl was a fertility goddess associated with dead souls who were thought to show themselves as magnificent black butterflies. In the poem's opening paragraph, her proud memory struggles against her present sadness. She celebrates her former beauty, power, and joyful energy; for instance, 'The eagle throbbed in my belly. I was the mountain that creates you as it dreams, the house of fire, the primordial pot where man is cooked and becomes man.' Yet she feels the deadening effect of her transformation from an active life force to a passive icon, surviving only in the substituted form of the Virgin of Guadalupe as a grey, insignificant statue in a cathedral courtyard. Tired of standing alone and cold in the shadow of the church, Itzpapálotl asks for 'a chair and a little sun'. Nonetheless, Paz's work of memory throughout the poem sustains a positive tone in the reader's mind. This is true of the poem's second paragraph where, in spectacular surreal images characteristic of Paz's style, the voice of the displaced goddess recalls her vibrant physicality and her elemental role in the creative cycles of nature; for instance, 'I was the flint that rips the storm clouds of night and opens the door of the showers.'

In the poem's third paragraph, Itzpapálotl returns to her painful experiences of the present – 'Each night is an eyelid the thorns never stop piercing' – in which visitors to the courtyard tiresomely and routinely toss coins and beads at her feet. She envies other creatures that can change their being, like the snake that sheds its skin. In the fourth paragraph, she calls to be reborn by being replanted in the earth. In a series of appropriately agricultural and strikingly erotic images, she desires to be sunned and rained upon, to be 'sown among the battle dead', for her body to be 'plowed' and turned into a field whose harvest will be richly reaped. In the short final paragraph, she speaks, like an expectant lover, of waiting for 'you' (which I take to mean both the land and people of Mexico) to 'open her body', there 'to read the inscription of your fate'. Paz's poem thus ends on a hopeful, prophetic note, full of possible reconciliation and renewal of life.

In this sense, we may take 'Obsidian butterfly' as both a reminder of the richness of the pre-Columbian world and a meditation on the hybrid nature of modern Mexican identity. Paz argues in lyrical manner for a synthesis of pagan and Christian cultures, one that would permit a sense of continuous rather than fractured or divided national history, and one that would challenge the idea of that history as comprehensible only in post-Conquest terms. In *The Labyrinth of Solitude*, Paz asks us 'to admit that when the Spaniards arrived in Mexico they found complete and refined civilizations', evidence of 'the vitality of pre-Cortesian cultures'. The poem is thus not anti-Catholic or anti-European; rather, Paz laments the suppression of a vital figure in traditional culture and regrets the lost history of his native land. After all, 60 per cent of the Mexican population remain *mestizo*, that is, of mixed Spanish and Indian descent. In his Nobel Lecture, Paz describes his responsibility as a writer to rehabilitate this forgotten past:

> In Mexico, the Spaniards encountered history as well as geography. That history is still alive: it is a present rather than a past. The temples and gods of pre-Columbian Mexico are a pile of ruins, but the spirit that breathed life into that world has not disappeared; it speaks to us in the hermetic language of myth, legend, forms of social coexistence, popular art, customs. Being a Mexican writer means listening to the voice of that present, that presence. Listening to it, deciphering it, expressing it.

For Paz therefore, any attempt to recover a lost sense of national identity – and thus eliminate what he calls the 'solitude' and 'silence' that haunt the Mexican consciousness – must start by recognizing the continuing value and significance of all the cultural and spiritual traditions that have made the history of his native land.

As for Castellanos, her work focuses on two areas long overlooked in Mexican literature: the racial and cultural oppression of indigenous peoples, and the situation of women in urban and rural Mexico. Chiapas had long been a site of conflict between landowners and indigenous peoples, and so it is unsurprising that she draws widely on the life and history of her native region. Her fiction is full of strangely skewed personal relationships, of downtrodden peasants and Indians, of female characters – wives, daughters, servants – trapped and frustrated by a suffocating provincial combination of church, class, and *machismo*. Most of these women are lonely, unhappy, often selfish or cruel, yet forced to keep up appearances. Most of them too strive ingeniously and sometimes desperately to throw off their physical and mental shackles.

Castellanos thus achieved recognition as a strongly feminist author and as one who broke both with European literary models and with the exotic stereotypes of native Mexican life that had characterized indigenist writing since the 1930s. Though she was involved at times in the activities of the *indigenismo* movement, she distanced herself from its literary label, as her subtle language, psychological complexity, dark humour, and careful approach to form contrasted starkly with the often-cartoonish realism of nativist prose.

'Death of the tiger' comes from a 1960 collection of nine stories, her second, entitled *Ciudad Real*, a collection also linked thematically to her second novel *Book of Lamentations* (*Oficio de tinieblas*, 1962), which is about an 1867 Chamula uprising in Chiapas. Ciudad Real is an old name for the town of San Cristóbal de las Casas. In a 1966 essay entitled *An Attempt at Self-Criticism*, Castellanos writes that *Ciudad Real*:

> ... compiles an inventory of the elements that make up one of the components of Mexican national reality wherein descendants of the conquered Indians live side by side with descendants of the conquering Europeans. If the former have lost the memory of their greatness, the latter have lost the attributes of their strength, and they all conflict in total decadence.

This state of affairs is very much the case in 'Death of the tiger', which, unlike 'Obsidian butterfly', reserves no place for coexistence, compromise, or reconciliation. Rather, it is a tragic story of long drawn-out persecution and ultimate destruction of an entire Indian tribe, the Bolometic, at the hands of the conquistadors and their white or *mestizo* descendants. Suffused with irony, the story describes how the Bolometic could not survive anywhere. If they stayed in the mountains, they would die; if they left, they would still die. The story also mirrors their painful decline in the corresponding moral and intellectual decline of their oppressors themselves.

The Bolometic lived proudly in the mountains of Chiapas under their *waigel* or protecting spirit, which was the tiger. But they already had sown the seeds of their eventual destruction by their own arrogance and sense of invulnerability. When the Spanish invaders arrived, the Bolometic were no match for them, and those who survived the sword took refuge in the foothills. There 'they began a precarious life in which the memory of past greatness slowly vanished, and history became a dying fire that no one was capable of rekindling'. The image of a dying fire symbolizes both the death of a noble culture and a constant battle against the cold that became one of their severest torments. No longer capable of asserting themselves as warriors, a sense of defeatism set in, and they endured centuries of misery and starvation. When the situation became intolerable, the men decided finally to leave their families in the windswept dwelling-place on the hillside and make their way down to Ciudad Real. Castellanos's irony moves into high gear as she describes the stagnant isolation of this colonial city, formerly vibrant, that had become 'a presumptuous and empty shell' through the complacency of its citizens and their social establishment.

On arrival in the city, the Bolometic were perplexed by the lack of vigorous life in such an architecturally beautiful and materially plentiful setting. They looked on with amazement at the scenes before their eyes. Drawn by an atavistic recognition of spiritual places, the destitute band of forty Indians entered a church to rest. There they were approached by a labour agent, Juvencio Ortiz, who

Rosario Castellanos

offered them work on a coffee plantation on the coast in full knowledge that they would be unlikely to survive the change in altitude and climate. With no choice but to accept Don Juvencio's offer, they headed for the coast, a descent that shattered their eardrums. Castellanos begins an intensely ironic climax: 'When the Bolometic reached the sea, they thought that its immense fury was mute.' Still suffering from the cold, now deafened too, the few that survived this final ordeal became so indebted to their new masters that they could never hope to return. In what remained of their hearing 'there echoed, more and more faintly, the voices of their women, calling them, and of their children, dying out. The tiger in the hills was never heard of again.'

Castellanos and Paz each share a strong awareness of Mexican history as well as a magic realist sensibility that draws on legend, folklore, and in the case of 'Death of the tiger', traditional storytelling techniques. However, their conclusions in these two texts are very different. Even while it is a lament for the loss of native tradition and belief, Paz's poem gives cause for certain optimism. The poem's dialectic, clearly discernible beneath a dazzling succession of surreal images, invites a reconciliatory synthesis of indigenous and European cultures. Castellanos's story, by contrast, tells only of endless separation and loss, of decay of both indigenous and settler cultures, of a historical reality that cannot be denied, of a wrong that cannot be righted even by the alchemical skills of these two accomplished masters of their literary art.

Virginia Haggard writing

9

A gentlewoman abroad: Virginia Haggard

On glancing at her biography, we might take Virginia Haggard to fit neatly into that well-worn category of a woman in whom our interest lies mainly in the greater or lesser male celebrities whom she partnered for substantial periods of her and their lives. There were also those whom she knew through family association, her own education, and her partners. But this given of celebrity by association is, as many feminist studies have shown, woefully inadequate in understanding the identity and the character of the woman herself. For there is a sense in which the story of her own life and artistic aspiration, realized in her photography and writing, is every bit as intriguing as the account of her relationships with dominant male figures – her father Godfrey Haggard; her great-uncle the novelist Rider Haggard; her brother, the writer and actor Stephen Haggard; her husbands and partners, the Scottish painter John McNeil, the Belgian photographer Charles Leirens, and the Belgian filmmaker Henri Storck; and above all the Russian painter Marc Chagall.

Virginia's English family was rooted in the landed gentry and the higher professional class. William Meybohm Haggard (1817–1893) was a barrister who became squire of Bradenham Hall in West Norfolk. A larger than life figure, he sired seven sons and three daughters, 'all Empire builders and forceful characters', according to Virginia. Somewhat against expectation, his youngest son eventually became a literary celebrity. He was Sir Henry Rider Haggard (1856–1925), who retired in 1882 to the home of his wife Louisa (Louie) Margitson at Ditchingham in South Norfolk, there to write most notably a series of full-blooded and mysterious adventure tales – such as the novels *She*, *King Solomon's Mines*, and *Alan Quartermain* – which were among the best-selling works of British fiction in the late nineteenth century. One of Rider's brothers, Alfred, took a high post in the Indian Civil Service but resigned in humiliation after publishing a severe critique of British imperialism on the subcontinent. One of Alfred's sons, Godfrey, Virginia's father, also forged a career – successfully in his case – in the Foreign Service.

Virginia was born in Paris on 19 July 1915 during her father's posting there as vice-consul. She had a great deal in common with her great-uncle Rider and her grandfather Alfred, taking an aptitude for the artistic life from the former and a nonconformist attitude from the latter. One meaning of the word 'haggard' is an 'untamed hawk', and from an early age Virginia asserted her 'wildness' in an individuality that resisted the accepted outlook and behaviour of both her family and her social class. Her father, with whom she had a love-hate relationship, described her as 'unaccommodating' and 'difficult to deal with along the ordinary lines'. In her journal, written with the benefit of a lifetime's hindsight, she expresses her remorse for having been 'a difficult daughter, a disloyal, even treacherous one'. She further writes of an inferiority complex she developed 'from feeling insignificant in [her parents'] lives as the youngest and more or less unwanted one'. This complex later plagued her relationships with men in her life, and particularly with McNeil and Chagall.

As a young woman thoroughly out of step with the conventions and values of her background, she chose to study art in the free academies that burgeoned in Montparnasse in the interwar years. At the Académie Scandinave her teachers Charles Dufresne and Marcel Gromaire – the one 'lyrical and imaginative', the other 'gloomy and severe' – were barely celebrities but were recognized as influential figures in the Parisian art world. However, it was as a student at the English engraver William Hayter's Atelier 17 that Virginia came across three genuine celebrities – Joan Miró, Max Ernst, and Alberto Giacometti. Coincidentally and courtesy of her father's position, she first met Chagall in 1933, briefly and formally in the stiff context of a British embassy reception, but did not see him again until a chance 1945 encounter, with momentous consequences.

Stephen Haggard persuaded their father that Virginia would benefit from exposure to the cultural life of London, in which he was already a shooting star, so she moved there from Paris. A loner nonetheless seeking safety in numbers, she opted for collective work, and landed a theatrical scene-painting job in a Cricklewood studio. The only woman there, she met the painter and theatrical designer-producer John McNeil and soon joined his experimental theatre project in Glasgow. In 1939, with the Second World War looming, London life growing more dangerous, and Virginia pregnant, Godfrey Haggard, by then consul-general in New York, arranged for the couple to seek refuge in the United States. This family largesse – in the form of influence, accommodation, and money – allowed them to get by, though precariously, in wartime Manhattan. But the relationship between John and Virginia, always stormy, grew unbearably so, and his domination of her repressed the stirrings of her own artistic talent. The stereotypical narrative of a woman's talent sacrificed to the service of a man's own career fits here, and was later repeated on a larger stage with Chagall. Virginia's two memoirs, *My Life with Chagall: Seven Years of Plenty with the Master as Told by the Woman Who Shared Them* (1986) and the posthumously published *Lifeline* (2009, edited by her daughter Jean McNeil), speak loudly to her frustration and resentment amid the moments of happiness she experienced in her life first with McNeil and then with Chagall.

Another artistic male against whom Virginia had to measure herself long before the ups and downs of her relationships with McNeil and Chagall was Stephen, a gifted, passionate, yet mercurial and demanding man to whom Virginia was very close. 'One had to be his disciple', she wrote in a foreshadowing of her later experiences. For a while in Paris and London of the 1930s, Virginia saw a lot of

Stephen, and began vicariously to experience the thrills as well as the letdowns, the trappings as well as the traps, of fame and reputation. His tragically brief life ending in the Arab world, he had the charisma of T. E. Lawrence on a minor scale, and Virginia saw in his artistic and individualistic make-up something of a kindred spirit. Olivia Manning based the character of Aidan Sheridan on him in her novel *Fortunes of War*. Virginia's relationship with her brother was her first brush with artistic celebrity, since he won a brilliant reputation especially on the stage and in the progressive literary circles of the 1930s. After saying goodbye to him in Piccadilly Circus on the eve of her departure for New York, Virginia never saw Stephen again. His death on a train from Cairo to Jerusalem in 1943, while working for British intelligence in Egypt, was apparently associated with a compli-cated Middle Eastern love affair and is accepted now as suicide. This event affected Virginia deeply, and more especially at a time when her marriage to McNeil was barely surviving. His loss deprived her of another Haggard who had offered her a mirror image of her own intellectual and social restlessness.

For a twenty-year period (roughly 1932 to 1952) Virginia was under the sway of three dominant men: Stephen Haggard, John McNeil, and Marc Chagall. For half of that time she was also occupied by the duties of motherhood to the two children she bore to McNeil and Chagall. It is not difficult to understand her inability to give rein to her own creative impulses. Moreover, it was not easy for a woman to establish herself in a male-dominated art world. Already in the years leading up to the outbreak of war, she 'had long since abandoned [her] dreams of becoming a painter'. Her natural shyness and subordination to her brother and her partners further served to thwart her desire to assert herself and live according to her own code of conduct and sense of freedom.

It may be stretching a point to consider John McNeil as a celebrity, but it is fair to say that at his best – that is, when free from depressive states – he cut a charismatic figure in the intensely politicized culture of Britain in the 1930s. His working-class background had made him into something of a 'Red Clydesider', who fervently believed that his mission as an artist was to make art and culture every bit as available to persons of a similar background to his as they were to the privileged sector of society that had spawned the likes of Virginia. She, always in latent if not blatant revolt from her class and its values, sympathized with his outlook on life. Excited by his ideologically driven aesthetic zeal and compas-sionate toward his insecure artistic temperament, she threw in her lot with him, perhaps partly to spite her family. Stephen, notwithstanding his own left-leaning idealism and romantic self-image, hated seeing his sister led by a magnetic but fundamentally unsuitable lover.

After the birth of Jean in New York in April 1940, it became more difficult for Virginia to try to extricate herself from a marriage that was slowly and inexorably becoming mutually destructive. Though heavily dependent on his wife, McNeil had an 'unconscious urge to humiliate' her, possibly on account of a hidden class resentment. 'Having a victim', she writes, 'had become as much of an addiction for him as being one was for me.' By her own admission too, Virginia became a drudge, a mere bystander to his obsessive and increasingly solitary artistic projects. She 'began to ... wilt like an unwatered plant' and sank into a 'state of non-existence', with only Jean to give her a measure of strength and self-respect. Plunged into depression, McNeil could no longer work, so Virginia became the breadwinner by cleaning the houses of well-heeled New Yorkers.

In the course of this menial occupation, she met Chagall again. A refugee too from the war in Europe, he was living on Riverside Drive in Manhattan. Grieving the loss of his beloved wife Bella during the war, he was finding it difficult to work or to feel at ease in his new surroundings. Moreover, he was never particularly fond of metropolitan life, remaining at heart a boy from the village-like Jewish quarter of Vitebsk. He was 58, Virginia was 30. It reminds us of Max Ernst, who was 46 when he met Leonora Carrington in 1937; she was 19.

After they became lovers, Virginia and Chagall moved to the sleepy hamlet of High Falls, nestling on the Shawangunk Ridge where the Hudson River valley rises to meet the eastern edge of the Catskill Mountains of New York. Their two years spent together there from the spring of 1946 to the summer of 1948 were among his happiest, all the more so when he fathered a son David by her. Since Virginia was still married – as much as he may have wished to, Chagall could not acknowledge David as an illegitimate child – David took the name of McNeil. Sharing a new family life with Virginia, Jean, and David helped Chagall recover from the loss of Bella. Benefiting from a monthly retainer from the Pierre Matisse gallery in New York City, he entered a productive period, one that was bolstered by the tranquil and beautiful landscape surrounding him.

Counting under 700 residents, High Falls seemingly remains much the same today. In a late September Indian summer, I found my way to the Emporium, a small and attractively designed business complex built from the remains of a motor vehicle service station. It included a gallery space where several local enthusiasts had installed a 'Chagall in High Falls' exhibit following its debut at the nearby Delaware and Hudson Canal Museum, a former Episcopal chapel on Mohonk Road. The canal, famous for the early conveying of anthracite coal from North-Eastern Pennsylvania to New York City, defines the history of High Falls as well as being directly related to the establishment of a spectacular resort hotel, the Mohonk Mountain House, built from the 1870s to 1910 atop the Shawangunk Ridge and still operating today. High Falls became a departure point via carriage for canal and rail travellers destined for the hotel.

Across from the museum, I found Wired Gallery, where over a pot of delicately flavoured tea the gallerist Sevan Melikyan shared with me his own enthusiasm for Chagall and Virginia's brief idyll. They had lived in a still-standing blue wood-framed house a little farther down Mohonk Road. Having toured the region, the exhibit I had seen at the Emporium is now housed in Wired. In this way, High

Falls – also home to the Polish exile artist and architect Jan Sawka from 1977 to his death in 2012 – is able to keep the couple's local flame alight.

Among their visitors was Charles Leirens; one of his photographs shows Chagall tickling a cow's nose, another ambling with David along a country road. These images, like others from the time, suggest a man deeply contented with a simple rural existence which both inspired him to paint and reminded him reassuringly of his Belarussian origins.

It was a satisfying life for Virginia too. Freed from her tormented relationship with McNeil, she regained her mental and physical health. She was Chagall's muse, and in that capacity began to dream anew of her own work. Ironically, as this desire to express herself grew stronger, it began to drive a wedge between them, one that resulted eventually in their separation. Yet it was he who demanded *her* sacrifice to *his* art, while she had hoped for a more reciprocally rewarding partnership. Her relationship with Chagall thus began to reflect the one with McNeil, but with a major difference: Virginia, a proud mother of two bright and bonny children, had now rediscovered her own identity. The old Haggard wild streak reappeared, and with it an unwillingness on her part to be forced into a mould in which she would again be little more than the passive partner of a self-absorbed man, as charming or affectionate as he might often be.

Overall, the High Falls years were fulfilling for both. It was on return to Europe in 1948 that the cracks in their life together grew visible. Chagall adopted more and more the attitude and bearing of the famous artist he had become, one in friendly rivalry with Pablo Picasso and Henri Matisse for the highest esteem in the European art world. And though they settled in Vence, in Provence, the glamorous attraction of the Parisian scene grew stronger for him, along with its demands for his visibility. Virginia felt lost in the shuffle, which at times resembled a stampede, of visitors, critics, curators, dealers, and other artists all keen to have an exchange with the master. As his secretary, Virginia acted capably, but only as long as she could remain offstage. Furthermore, she felt excluded from his Yiddish- and Russian-speaking circles, and complained of his lack of warmth and commitment to her. 'He talked a lot about love in general', she remembers, 'he painted love, but he didn't practise it.' As he distanced himself from her and preoccupied himself with his work and his place in the cultural pantheon, so Leirens paid her increasing attention until, inevitably perhaps, a love affair blossomed between them. This turn of events brought out the worst of Chagall's chronic insecurity and jealousy. Enraged by the affair, he chastised her physically and mentally, until she left him in 1952 for Leirens and a new life, first in Paris, then in Brussels. Chagall had wanted her to play an unsuitable role, one moreover in which she was uninterested, that of the publicly supportive 'trophy' wife of a famous artist. She resented his attempt to make her a replacement for Bella or for his daughter Ida, who had long acted as his agent.

Four months after their break-up, Chagall married his new secretary, Valentina

(Vava) Brodsky, a worldly émigré Russian Jewess at ease in mainstream culture. For him, she checked all the boxes that Virginia had not done. There seems little doubt that Chagall had loved Virginia, but his celebrity status and her growing self-assertiveness ultimately came between them. It may strike us as strange, though almost predictable, that in writings about the artist before Sidney Alexander's 1978 biography, no mention is made of Virginia, despite her having almost singlehandedly brought him back from an emotional and artistic brink. The main reason for Virginia having been written out of the Chagall history was the role played by Vava, whose mission, eagerly supported by the French cultural establishment, was to turn Chagall into a 'French' rather than a 'Russian Jewish émigré' artist. She largely succeeded in that mission, as his celebrity grew to match that of Picasso and Matisse.

Encouraged and taught by Leirens, with whom she enjoyed a brief but happy marriage following her divorce from McNeil, Virginia took up photography and grew accomplished in the art. Following his death in 1963, she took over his commission, begun in 1958, of photographing Belgian writers, painters, sculptors, and musicians for the national Ministry of Education. Other commissions followed, including one from the Belgian royal family, but she also sought out her own subjects; Jean remembers her successfully approaching Marcel Marceau. Her method of portraiture was discreet and self-effacing; it demonstrated a finely tuned detachment from her subjects as well as a flexible accommodation to them. She also liked to contextualize her portraits, whether by way of an artist's workplace or an appropriate landscape in which to place her subject. Virginia disliked the vogue of technical experiment for its own sake or of self-consciously stylized work. In her own words, she strove rather to create 'an honestly independent point of view, something personal and vital and true'. The quality of her work was recognized in a 2001 exhibition at the Museum of Photography in Charleroi, Belgium, accompanied by a catalogue (*Virginia Haggard-Leirens*) of some of her best images.

After losing Leirens, Virginia became the companion of another Belgian artist, the documentary filmmaker Henri Storck, who was enjoying a lengthy and highly reputed career and with whom she lived happily in Brussels until his death in 1999. It was toward the end of that period that I met her for the only time, while interviewing Storck at their home on rue Groeselenberg in the suburb of Uccle, during research for *Split Screen*, my history of Belgian cinema. Their house, a former sculptor's studio which they had acquired in 1970, was spacious and secluded. Storck was a gracious host, Virginia likewise. Charming and vivacious, she was remarkably youthful looking for her age, tall and graceful, and still possessing the willowy figure that is so striking in photographs of her earlier life.

As did Leirens before him, Storck encouraged and supported her artistic aspirations. He built on her photographic skills by teaching her the arts of cinematic lighting and on-set photography, and she made a major contribution to his final films by taking all his preproduction and production stills. By the late 1980s, however, she had almost given up professional photography, and for the rest of her life she turned her attention to writing.

'Almost all of my life I have been *preparing* to write', runs a 1996 journal entry. She had grown tired not only of the physical demands of developing and printing photographs, but also of its demanding interactions with others. The privacy and relative ease of writing appealed more to her. Thus, as she puts it, 'my darkroom has become a light room'. Nonetheless, in 1980, as she mulled over ideas for an as yet unpublished novel, *The Spare Room*, she could still conceive of writing in terms of visual art: 'It's the first time I have found a sort of canvas onto which I can paint some of the material I have collected.' Her thoughts took 'interesting shapes' through writing. As with her photography, so with her writing: one must be not only passionate and humorous but also 'completely truthful'.

Virginia lived on in Brussels until her own death in 2006 at the age of 91. A documentary film interviewing her at home and focusing on her photographic work was made by André Colinet in 2004. In *Lifeline*, she turns to her origins, upbringing, and family relationships until the start of the Second World War years. In 2017, Jean McNeil edited a book of Virginia's journal entries entitled *Groeselenberg Diaries 1970–1997*. This collection offers fascinating insights into Virginia's self-discovery through writing. She is casual about dating her entries, but this may be seen as a deliberate effort to remove herself from the coordinates of daily life in order to lose herself in her own work. 'To write I must be cut off,' she states, something that even the supportive Leirens and Storck failed sometimes to understand, not least her desire, seemingly acceptable for males, to write alone in cafés.

My Life with Chagall came out when Virginia was 71 years old. Two years after its publication she acknowledged in her journal that she 'was scared of being inadequate. Now my book gives me conviction in myself.' In its final pages, she describes losing the remorse she felt at having left Chagall; this loss occurred on realizing that Chagall's life, which lasted until he was 97 and still painting, had turned out in the way it seemed destined to do: fame, fortune, a devoted family, and artistic fulfilment. One wonders if he would have survived to enjoy all that had it not been for Virginia saving him at a time when he teetered on the edge of self-destruction. As for Virginia, another Haggard willing to swim against the tide of expectation for the sake of her own deeply felt convictions and way of doing things, she finally comes into her own despite the challenges of an ageing body and mind. In 1991 she writes in her journal, 'I have been blown about a lot by my four husbands. Finally I have found my own direction.'

In late October 2018, a couple of years after my initial visit, I found myself heading again to High Falls. The last of the yellows and reds of fall were fading gently. On front porches, pumpkins piled up amid scarecrows and skeletons. Virginia's story had entered a new dimension and drawn me back to Wired Gallery. 'The Virginia Project' is a reinterpretation of her and her daughter Jean's experiences in High Falls by writer Tina Barry and fourteen female visual artists, each responding freely to various of Barry's prose poems. In this intimate space, Virginia had finally taken centre stage. Now it was *her* expatriate life in the United States, rather than that of Marc Chagall, that this exhibition celebrated; for the moment, at least, she had become the celebrity.

10

Change and the modern churchman:
J. K. Nettlefold

While sorting through my late mother's possessions at her house in Norwich, England, I came upon two books of memoirs, *Unusual Partners* (1956) and *From a Country Rectory* (1958) by J. K. Nettlefold, rector of Bourton-in-the-Water, Gloucestershire, in the English Cotswold country. The author had inscribed each volume to his friend, my grandfather Alexander Hattrell, a lawyer and citizen of the abbey town of Tewkesbury, Gloucestershire where Nettlefold spent his retirement in the 1960s. The copy of *Unusual Partners* contained both a clipping of a review by (Sir) John Betjeman in the national press (one that shared space with reviews of biographies of Charles Dickens and H. G. Wells) and a copy of a 24 July 1956 letter to Nettlefold. In his review, Betjeman writes of gaining 'the same pleasure as I have had from the poet Cowper's letters. It is written without sentiment, with utter honesty and with an Attlee-like flatness which is at once engaging and readable.' In his letter, presumably responding to one from Nettlefold, Betjeman reassures the author that his reference to the style of former British Prime Minister Clement Attlee, whose autobiography *As It Happened* had appeared in 1954, is 'a compliment, because dear old Attlee is my hero and he does write entirely without adjectives like you, and I like your style and find it neither wearisome nor tiresome'. He exhorts Nettlefold not to 'go in for fine literary flourishes', as 'the whole point of your style is its staccato simplicity, and that's partly what makes the book so enjoyable'.

The subject of the first memoir, *Unusual Partners*, is Nettlefold's unlikely thirty-year relationship with an adopted 'aunt', Alexandra Mary Von Bosse, a woman of Irish origin married into Russian and German society, whom he had met in Dresden in 1922. The author's focus on his aunt's powerful presence and personal attributes offers him a degree of aesthetic distance, yet the book indirectly tells much of Nettlefold's own curious story of personal and spiritual development in the light of modern social and theological change. The second memoir, *From a Country Rectory*, is a set of essays in the British parson-author tradition on various aspects of Nettlefold's personal and pastoral life. The majority of its chapters are of less historical interest than those of the first volume, though two of them give valuable insight into Nettlefold's earlier career.

As Betjeman's remarks suggest, the interest of Nettlefold's memoirs lies less in any marked literary talent than in a refreshing and entertaining address to the common reader and in an embodiment of 'history from below', in this case a lively panorama

J. K. Nettlefold on his graduation, 1921

of English social and ecclesiastical life during the first half of the twentieth century. Betjeman's review also indicates how important he felt it was to notice interesting and well-designed books produced by provincial publishers whose often-distinctive output the metropolitan press might otherwise ignore. Such a publisher, Edward J. Burrow & Company, of Cheltenham, Gloucestershire, published Nettlefold's two books.

My trailing of Nettlefold thus led me to Burrow (1869–1935) upon whom I merely touch here. Trained as a chemist and pharmacist, he was a master draughtsman-etcher, author, and archaeologist, who established his own printing company in 1900 to produce picture postcards and his own books. An accomplished pianist and theatregoer, Burrow was a fellow of the Royal Society of Arts and a governor of the Shakespeare Memorial Theatre (now Royal Shakespeare Company). His original company, extant today in a corporate form that might have raised its idealistic founder's eyebrows, was a profit-sharing collective of 350 artists. Burrow sensed a growing market for tourist information and in 1904 published the first *Burrow's Guide*, to Cheltenham. By the 1930s the series carried 500 titles. Among other established series were city maps; from my own youth I recall them for their unusual use of a movable pointer. The Burrow brand became synonymous with artistically designed and reliable publications.

Named for the Unitarian theologian, historian, and philologist John Kenrick (1788–1877), J. K. (Ken) Nettlefold was born on 30 October 1897 to a prominent Birmingham family of Unitarians. Nonconformists such as the Nettlefolds were prominent among Victorian entrepreneurs, as they had also been during the 'Midlands Enlightenment' of the previous century when socially conscious men like Josiah Wedgwood, Joseph Priestley, James Watt, and Erasmus Darwin gave scientific and ethical inspiration to the nascent Industrial Revolution. The family firm of Nettlefolds Ltd. began by making fasteners. It was taken over in 1902 to become part of Guest, Keen & Nettlefolds, a renowned company (now the multinational GKN) that manufactured screws, nuts, and bolts in Birmingham, 'the workshop of the world'. Ken's father, John Sutton Nettlefold (1866–1930), was a pioneering town planner with a special interest in housing and social issues; notable among his books are *Slum Reform and Town Planning* (1906) and *Practical Housing* (1908). The family lived in Birmingham at Beechenhurst House from 1891 to 1904, and at Winterbourne House from 1904 to 1919, a residence that John Sutton commissioned local architect Joseph Lancaster Ball to design in the Arts and Crafts style. Now owned by the University of Birmingham, Winterbourne's gates and doors are open to the public.

After a public-school education at Marlborough College, Nettlefold served in the First World War as a junior officer stationed in Salonika, Greece with the Third Wessex Brigade of the Royal Field Artillery. I find it tempting to imagine that he may have encountered the composer Ralph Vaughan Williams, who was also stationed there with the Royal Army Medical Corps. Resigning his commission in 1920, Nettlefold studied first at Oxford University, taking a BA degree at Balliol College, then at the London School of Economics, and then back in Oxford at Manchester College, a dissenting academy where he trained for the Unitarian ministry. During the summer vacation of 1922, he met his 'aunt' in Dresden; the narrative of *Unusual Partners* begins with that meeting. In 1923, the Unitarian Church appointed him to its ministry at Stockport ('Stockley' in the memoir, and presumably an instance of intentional distancing rather than failed memory) near Manchester where his 'aunt' joined him several months later. They were to be inseparable companions for the next thirty years.

The story of their friendship is extraordinary, but I am interested more in Nettlefold and in the challenges that he faced as a young man trying to find himself, his faith, and his way in the world. In the first chapter of *Unusual Partners*, he describes himself as a 'lame dog' whom his 'aunt' helped 'to become stronger in health and more independent', as she had done for many others. It emerges that he had a difficult relationship with his family, and especially with his mother Margaret, who had hoped he would enter business in true Nettlefold style. He acknowledges reaching the edge of a nervous breakdown, to which the constraints of a stuffy family life still functioning along rigidly old-fashioned lines may have contributed. Whether active service at the tender age of 19 also contributed to his nervousness is unclear but entirely possible. Letters home he wrote from Greece, a number of which Winterbourne House holds in its archive, do not offer any evidence of a traumatic experience in the line of duty, but neither do they offer a full account of his war years.

At the same time, he was beginning to question his religious faith and ecclesiastical identity. Exposure to elements of radical theology at Manchester College may have played a part in his rethink, while in one chapter of *From a Country Rectory* he describes the effect on him, while an army cadet in 1916, of hearing two liberal preachers blessed with strong personalities and performative gifts. In writing that he attended 'James's Chapel' in an unnamed town where he was billeted (and which is certainly Exeter, Devon), his intentional distancing may have functioned again, as the 'Demolition Exeter' website reveals that a James's Meeting existed from 1687 to 1760 before being replaced by a new chapel, George's Meeting, in close proximity to it. Though the older meeting house still stood in 1916, he would have therefore attended George's Meeting where one of the two preachers, the Rev. Robert Henry Underwood Bloor, was minister at the time.

The other preacher was the Rev. Thomas William Chignell ('Chilwell' in Nettlefold's narrative), who was Bloor's predecessor at George's Meeting for over forty years. He found much to enthuse over in Chignell's and Bloor's sermons, especially as both were literary men. A great admirer of Carlyle and Goethe, Chignell 'preached from them almost as much as he preached from the Bible'. Moreover, he used his own hymn book (officially designated 'P' for 'peculiar' by the Unitarian Church) in which many of the hymns (often altered or added to by Chignell) were excerpts from poems by Wordsworth, Tennyson, and Browning. Likewise of Bloor, Nettlefold writes, 'he loved good books, and as one listened to him, he made one love them too'. This praise becomes clearer on noting Bloor's own books, which include *The English Novel from Chaucer to Galsworthy* (1935) and *Christianity and the Religious Drama* (1930).

Nettlefold's inspiring experience at Exeter only served to heighten his desire to break the shackles of his upbringing:

This unexpectedness, this unconventionality, fascinated me and knocked me off my balance. I was just 19, an age when one begins to try to think one's own thoughts and make one's own experiments. And it was 1916. The Victorian age was coming to an end. The Victorian age means to me the family circle. I belonged to a very large one .... It was stifling; as if there were a high wall round the family, separating them from the rest of mankind. ... and life within the wall was very dull .... The only right ways of living and thinking were the ways of the family .... I wanted to get outside the wall; I wanted to be at ease with the people I spoke to in the shops, and passed in the street. I wanted to know how they lived, and what they thought .... Some family pride is a good thing; but one can have too much.

Viewing his own family as intolerant, he learned the virtue of tolerance from Bloor, who partly influenced him to become a Unitarian minister. Unfortunately, though, he was largely unhappy in his time at Stockport, where 'the ugliness of everything was dreadful'. The smoky, grimy, dreary aspect of the town – redolent of Dickens's *Hard Times* written over sixty years earlier – depressed him as much as did the ground-down lives of many of its citizens. Despite his altruism, his desire to preach 'moral and spiritual values', and his wish to engage with a broader swathe of society, the 'innocent and inexperienced' Nettlefold discovered he was largely a fish out of water. Understandably, he began to question his decision to enter the ministry. His sparse congregation was often contentious, his predecessor as minister kept hovering annoyingly in the background, and he was beginning to search for a spiritual life that might better reflect his deeper aspirations and values. Some aspects of Unitarian worship did not sit well with him. A chapter in *From a Country Rectory* entitled 'Prayer in public worship' deals with the nonconformist 'long' prayer that 'is the minister's own composition, and ... sometimes extempore'. He found it tiresome and preferred prayer from a book, so despite its elaborate style and sentimental tone he used *The Ten Services*, an 1860 Unitarian compilation, for twelve years. By way of contrast, he praises *The Book of Common Prayer* for its conciseness and beauty, and we may thus understand the seeds of his attraction to Anglicanism.

Among the positives he took from his four years of soul-searching in Stockport was an ability to hear lectures by A. S. Peake (1865–1929), then professor of biblical exegesis at Manchester University. A Methodist, Peake taught the Bible 'according to the principles of modern historical study', so Nettlefold 'learnt to read it as a whole' as opposed to the piecemeal knowledge of it he had gained in boyhood. *A Commentary on the Bible* (1919), edited by Peake, is still used today.

He eventually requested a new charge, so the Church appointed him minister of the Octagon Chapel in Norwich. This was 'heaven' after Stockport. His new congregation was more serious and more placid, though his 'aunt' called it either 'half dead or asleep'. The meeting-house, designed by local architect Thomas Ivory and built by Presbyterians in 1756, is one of the most beautiful in England. As for his domestic life, number 4 Chapel Field North, one of the most elegant Regency houses in the city and originally built for a mayor of Norwich, became Nettlefold's home. It still overlooks Chapelfield Gardens, a small public park that serves as a priceless green lung in the heart of the city. Discovering his life in Norwich was a bonus for me in pursuing this subject, as I have ever admired both the Octagon Chapel and the house on Chapel Field from my own upbringing in the old cathedral city.

Members of his congregation noticed his 'growing tendency towards a more orthodox theology'. One member called him an 'Evangelical'. Nettlefold commented, 'He was right …. My thoughts were fixed more and more on Christ', though when he mentioned Christ in his sermon, 'a snort was sometimes heard from the choir'. He spent eight happy years in Norwich from 1927 to 1935, yet he remained restless to escape from a monotonous life there, one that 'was like living in a Jane Austen novel, without the love interest which is what keeps her novels going'. Mirroring his father's social mission, he found some alternative activity by involving himself in building small houses and apartments for old people in need, but it was his interest in the Modern Churchmen's Union, whose conferences he began to attend, that tipped him decisively toward a new religious affiliation.

The interwar years were vibrant ones for modernist theology as well as being the period of its proponents' fiercest debates with fundamentalists, a struggle epitomized by the 1925 Scopes trial in the United States over the teaching of evolution in schools. Founded by Anglicans in 1898, the Churchmen's Union for the Advancement of Liberal Religious Thought had mercifully shortened its name in 1928, while its periodical *The Modern Churchman* had become an influential organ. At the Union meetings, Nettlefold discovered a means of building theology onto his biblical knowledge. He read widely in modernist scholarship – for instance, Hastings Rashdall's rational doctrine of the Trinity – and it gave him answers to many of his questions. Though he describes leaving the Norwich chapel as 'very painful', he writes that he 'wanted a larger sphere, to be a member of a bigger Christian society' than the one offered him by the Unitarian Church.

Resigning from the Unitarian Ministry in 1935, he spent two years back in the Oxford area at Ripon Hall Modernist Theological College (now Ripon Cuddesdon College) in training for the Anglican ministry. Dr Henry Major, editor of *The Modern Churchman* and, writes Nettlefold, 'the most Christian man that I have known personally', was principal of the college at the time. Nettlefold was ordained in 1937, spent the next two years as a curate, and in 1939 became rector of Bitterley, a village near Ludlow, Shropshire. After the Second World War he married Phyllis Gertrude Barsley, though they had no children. Isolated in remote Bitterley, he moved again in 1948 to become rector of Bourton-on-the-Water, Gloucestershire, a much larger parish where he remained until his retirement in 1960. His 'aunt' died in 1952 after they had shared thirty years of unwavering mutual companionship. Ken Nettlefold died at home in Tewkesbury on 26 February 1969.

These memoirs also say much about his years as a Church of England minister, but those years are not pertinent to the theme of this essay. Above all, they tell a fascinating story both of the remarkable 'aunt' Von Bosse and of the author himself in his long quest for self-knowledge and spiritual fulfilment. It may be hard to claim any outstanding literary merit for the two books, but they are candid, lucid, liberally sprinkled with humour, and paint a vivid picture of English life at the time.

Ned Washington

11

Waxing lyrical: Ned Washington

Popular songwriting is a craft aspiring to an art. A deceptively simple task: writing a successful song demands a high level of concentration, skill, and practice. Ira Gershwin, who knew a thing or two about writing lyrics, figured it took 'four or five years collaborating with a knowledgeable composer to become a well-rounded lyricist'. The principal function of songwriting is to entertain a mass audience with a product that today may be consumed on records or computerized downloads, in the mass broadcast media of radio and television, and in theatres, concert venues, and clubs by way of stage shows or movies.

A popular song aspires to art when it transcends formula to become something beautiful or meaningful in itself. For a lyricist, the words must complement the music perfectly, and for a composer, vice versa. This combination is the key to a fully realized song. Hence the words of a song may look thin or banal when read on the page or spoken aloud, but they may enter another dimension in a felicitous conjunction with music. In the same way, a lyricist who treats his task as that of a literary poet will likely find his use of language to be unsuited to the musical purpose. Then again, as William Zinsser asserts in *Easy to Remember: The Great American Songwriters and Their Songs* (2001), 'poets, on the other hand, operate only in the service of poetry – which is why they don't generally make good lyricists'. Furthermore, there is always something vaguely absurd in scholars subjecting popular song lyrics to academic criticism and treating them as if they were purely literary creations. In the words of Stephen Sondheim, a master song craftsman, 'if poetry is the art of saying a lot in a little, lyric-writing is the art of finding the right balance between saying too much and not enough'.

The work of the lyricist falls mainly into two areas: writing independently of dramatic productions, or for them. The American history of writing lyrics inde-pendently of dramatic productions begins with the establishment of Tin Pan Alley as a commercial phenomenon following the popularity of a modified folk music for domestic and public consumption that Stephen Foster and others had created in the late nineteenth century. Tin Pan Alley revolved initially around the demand for sheet music publication, an output that survived as a retail business long after it was supplanted in popularity by the recorded music industry from the 1920s onward. In turn, the record industry was bolstered by radio, television, cinema, live performance in clubs and dance halls, and the placement of jukeboxes in cafés, bars, and restaurants.

In the case of writing lyrics for a musical production, a further distinction is to be made for both stage and screen between the song lyricist and the librettist, who writes the 'book' (the dramatic dialogue) for the musical drama in question. Following the development of modern musical theatre out of popular stage plays, vaudeville, burlesque, and European light opera, the history of writing lyrics for dramatic productions centred on Broadway, and from the late 1920s also on Hollywood, which rushed to acquire music publishing houses. By the end of the 1930s, says Ian Whitcomb in *After the Ball* (1972), 'over three quarters of the nation's hit songs were controlled by the movie business'.

Within the film world we may distinguish between the composition of songs for musicals and the presence of songs in nonmusical dramas. In the case of musicals, the songs are inevitably part of the story world (or diegesis) of the film. In the case of nonmusical dramas, we may discern three major song categories, the first two diegetic to a lesser or greater degree, and the third not so. The first category consists of incidental songs of little or no bearing on dramatic action that are presented merely as an opportunity for performance and for mood enhancement of a film. The second category, by contrast, consists of songs that contribute to the dramatic action of a film as well as to its themes or moods. The third category consists of title or theme songs that provide, says film scholar Rick Altman, 'a unique opportunity to editorialize and to focus audience attention'.

The city of Scranton, in North-East Pennsylvania, was once a leading producer of anthracite coal. On arriving in the area in 1988 to take up an academic position, I witnessed a formerly prosperous conurbation trying to revive itself after decades of postindustrial decline. One part of my growing curiosity about the history and culture of the city concerned its crop of artistic talent. Among writers, I came upon the poet W. S. Merwin, United States Laureate from 2010 to 2011, who had moved to Scranton from New York City at the age of 9; the comic strip writer Joe Gill, creator for Charlton Comics of such stirring characters as Captain Atom and Judomaster; the journalist Jane Jacobs, whose *The Death and Life of Great American Cities* (1961) was a milestone in urban studies; and Jason Miller, who moved to Scranton from New York City at the age of 2 and whose play *That Championship Season*, about a local high school basketball team, won a Pulitzer Prize in 1972. Miller is perhaps better remembered as playing the priest Father Damien in William Friedkin's infamous horror film *The Exorcist* (1973).

Then there was Ned Washington, born in Scranton in 1901. Of the nine children of Michael and Catharine Washington, Edward (Ned) was the only one *not* to have taken music lessons. However, he began early to be fascinated by the play of words, leading him as a youth to dabble in writing poems, a number of which were published in newspapers and magazines. From his pen flowed eventually a catalogue of beautiful, inventive, and heartfelt songs for the stage, for the music industry, and for both big and small screens. As a baby boomer raised on rock and roll (my parents, quite indulgent by nature, stopped short of banning my incessant plays of 'Great balls of fire' by Jerry Lee Lewis), many of those classic songs in their original popular incarnations had completely passed me by until I discovered them – along with much else in the Great American Songbook (What a GAS!) – on developing in adulthood a serious taste for modern jazz. Their lyrical and musical subtleties have lent themselves remarkably to all manner of creative interpretations by numerous jazz vocalists and instrumentalists. To trace Washington's songwriting career as well as the success of his best-known songs thus affords us a look into both the evolving patterns of American popular music and the corresponding changes in modes of representation and audience tastes throughout much of the twentieth century.

Behind every great song lies a great songwriter. Yet, unless the singer happens also to be the writer, as is more common today, it is usually the performer alone who is celebrated by the general public. Many accomplished songwriters thus risk being relatively unsung. As Ken Bloom suggests in *The American Songbook* (2005), though 'most people who care about American popular song are familiar with the giants of the field' – we think of household names such as George and Ira Gershwin, Richard Rodgers and Lorenz Hart, Jerome Kern, Irving Berlin, Cole Porter, and Duke Ellington – 'many worthy composers and lyricists remain completely unknown'. Washington, though given his due by those in the know, is a good case in point, the titles and melodies of his major songs striking more chords with most people than does his name. He is a distinctive figure too in that along with Porter, Johnny Mercer, Hoagy Carmichael, and a handful of others, he belonged to a Gentile minority in a profession heavily dominated by Jews.

The coming of the talkies around 1930 drew many authors, often famous ones like Ernest Hemingway and William Faulkner, to Hollywood as scriptwriters; it also gave lucrative opportunities to song composers and lyricists. These artists complemented those composers – mainly European émigrés from the operatic and orchestral traditions, such as Erich Wolfgang Korngold, Alfred Newman, and Max Steiner – whom the studios hired as musical directors of instrumental scores. Some of the New York-based songwriters – such as Berlin, Mercer, Harry Warren, and Jimmy Van Heusen – took kindly to West Coast life and worked extensively in Hollywood, while others – such as Rodgers, Hart, Porter, and the Gershwin brothers – did limited film work and remained closer to the Big Apple. And several one-time Hollywood stalwarts – such as Jule Styne and Frank Loesser – eventually shifted their base to Broadway.

Though work was plentiful in Hollywood and the money was good, the song-writers remained company hirelings without either the status or privileges of their lives in New York, where unlike in Hollywood they saw a share of the profits from their shows. In a practice that Rodgers called 'sheer suicide' for a composer, a studio would blithely pit several top-notch craftsmen against one another in order to pick the best song for its perceived needs. The crossover potential of a hit record was deemed more valuable than plot- or character-related songs. Many well-crafted songs were thus ignored or dropped as a result of dubious studio judgments. Two infamous and barely conceivable instances: Harold Arlen and Max Steiner's 'Over the rainbow' was dropped three times from *The Wizard of Oz* (1939), while in RKO's *The Gay Divorcée* (1934), 'Night and day' was the sole survivor of Cole Porter's entire score for the stage musical that it adapted.

❁ ❁ ❁

In 1922, having come of age, Ned Washington moved to New York City and worked in vaudeville as a master of ceremonies, as a booker of artists, and as a sketch writer for them. Bitten by the showbiz bug, he began to write lyrics for Broadway revues, for radio, and for the burgeoning record industry. Considerable rewards were on offer to aspiring songwriters who could interest a star performer in recording their material. In 1931, Washington and the composer Victor Young, with whom he would collaborate successfully on many subsequent occasions, persuaded torch singer Lee Wiley to record 'Got the South in my soul', a song quickly covered by the Boswell Sisters and Paul Robeson. With this hit, Ned Washington was off and running. Among the lyrics he wrote for Tin Pan Alley over the course of the next two years are three outstanding songs: '(I don't stand a) ghost of a chance (with you)' (music by Young); 'I'm getting sentimental over you' (music by George Bassman); and 'Smoke rings' (music by Gene Gifford).

'Ghost of a chance' landed Washington and Young their biggest fish so far, Bing Crosby. It was released as the B-side of Crosby's 'Just an echo in the valley', but the crooner took Washington's song to number five on the Hit Parade. Crosby was given co-writing credit, but it remains unclear how much, if any, he contributed to the song. It was common practice in those days to give credit to a star performer. The song was reprised notably in an instrumental version by Cab Calloway's Orchestra with Chu Berry on tenor saxophone in 1940, while more recently Linda Ronstadt and Diana Krall have added their names to a long list of artists who have interpreted this touching blend of sadness and hope.

George Bassman supposedly sold the rights to 'I'm getting sentimental over you' to the song publisher Irving Mills for a mere $25. Recorded as a foxtrot by Northeastern Pennsylvania's very own Dorsey Brothers band (they were from another coal town, Shenandoah), Tommy Dorsey chose the song as his own orchestra's theme tune in 1935. Count Basie, Ella Fitzgerald, Frank Sinatra, Oscar Peterson and many other famous musicians have covered it. Dorsey's version may be heard in two films set in the 1930s: Woody Allen's 1987 *Radio Days* and Steven Soderbergh's 1993 *King of the Hill*.

An ethereal and devilishly catchy song, 'Smoke rings' was promptly adopted as a theme tune by Glen Gray, the saxophonist-leader of the Casa Loma Orchestra, a popular and enduring swing band that played from 1927 to 1963. Some very different interpreters of this song include the Mills Brothers, the first African American pop/jazz vocal group to gain mass acceptance; multitracking electric guitar trailblazer Les Paul, who with his wife Mary Ford exploits the song's harmonies as deftly as did the Mills; soul music pioneer Sam Cooke; and K. D. Lang, who gives it a Hawaiian treatment.

As the coming of sound to the movies brought down the curtain on vaudeville, Washington duly signed with the Vitaphone Company to write lyrics for Warner Brothers pictures. 1929's 'Singin' in the bathtub' was his first success; performed by Winnie Lightner in *Show of Shows*, it was then waxed by Guy Lombardo and His Royal Canadians. In 1934, Washington moved to Hollywood to concentrate for much of his career on writing movie songs. Another early success was 'Cosi-cosa', which he penned for MGM's *A Night at the Opera* (1935), starring the three Marx Brothers (minus Zeppo for the first time), Margaret Dumont, Kitty Carlisle, and Allan Jones. A slight but infectiously uplifting song, 'Cosi-cosa' belongs to the diegesis of the film without bearing on the plot in any significant way. Encouraged by an overflowing spaghetti dinner (an influence, surely, on a similar scene in the Beatles' 1967 television comedy *Magical Mystery Tour*), three Italian stowaways on board an ocean liner bound for the United States perform the song for the steerage passengers. Chico Marx plays piano, Harpo (of course) plays harp, and Allan Jones sings. A twist on the old *funiculi-funicula* combination, *cosi-cosa* is equivalent to the classic French noncommittal phrase *comme ci, comme ça* meaning 'not good nor bad' or 'maybe yes, maybe no'. Its performance here is merely a musical interlude between gags, though it does imply an ambiguous situation facing the three – their bellies filled and halfway to America yet facing possible arrest and rejection in the end. The song has such an authentic ring that audiences still take it to be a genuine Neapolitan folk song rather than a spirited concoction distilled on the Hollywood lot by Washington along with composers Bronislaw Kaper and Walter Jurmann. As delightful a piece of fluff as it is, *Variety's* critic of the time placed it in perspective with the comment that 'songs in a Marx picture are generally at a disadvantage because they're more or less interruptions, the customers awaiting the next laugh'.

In 1937, Washington wrote the beautifully rhymed ballad 'The nearness of you', with music by Hoagy Carmichael, for *Romance in the Rough*, a film that was never made. Because of the similar titles, it has been wrongly assumed that the song was written for Paramount's operetta *Romance in the Dark* (1938), though actress and diva Gladys Swarthout does perform it in a film that has been all but forgotten. The song, however, is a gem in the Great American Songbook, having been popularized in 1940 by the Glenn Miller Band with vocalist Ray Eberle. Many other pop and jazz luminaries have recorded it, notably Sarah Vaughan in 1949 and more recently Norah Jones on her exceptional 2002 debut album *Come Away with Me*.

It was in his work for Disney at the beginning of the 1940s that Washington fully established his reputation as a songwriter for the movies. With the composers Leigh Harline and Paul J. Smith, he came up with the entire score of *Pinocchio*

(1940). This score won an Academy Award, as did Washington and Harline for the song 'When you wish upon a star'. The song barely enters the story world of the film; we may call it *meta*diegetic. We hear the song as a theme over the main credits before it enters the diegesis in the opening scene as sung by Pinocchio's pal Jiminy Cricket in the voice of Cliff Edwards. Immediately afterwards, Jiminy Cricket opens the book on the fairy story of Pinocchio, at which point we enter the primary diegesis with a panoramic establishing shot of a starlit town and surrounding mountains in sight of the toymaker Geppetto's house. The song returns outside the diegesis at the end, but in both instances has overarching thematic and narrative relevance. 'When you wish upon a star' was so successful that it became the trademark Disney theme song, and is still heard widely in connection with anything that bears the Disney brand. Other notable songs in *Pinocchio* include 'I've got no strings', 'Give a little whistle', and 'Hi-diddle-dee-dee (an actor's life for me)'. Firmly within the diegesis, they resemble 'When you wish upon a star' in standing nonetheless on their own merits while serving the narrative superbly. Incidentally, in a curious intertextual turn, 'When you wish upon a star' became a traditional Christmas song in Japan and Scandinavia, offering a remarkable synthesis of supernatural, fatalistic, and Christian visions.

Working with composers Frank E. Churchill and Oliver Wallace, Washington came up with another Disney score, for *Dumbo* (1941), from which the song 'Baby mine' was nominated for an Oscar. Two other notable songs from this film are 'When I see an elephant fly' and 'Pink elephants on parade'.

Washington thereafter resumed work for various studios, especially together with Victor Young. His forte became the composition of theme or title songs for films rather than of full scores. Paramount's *The Uninvited* (1944) is an underrated gothic noir, and Samuel Goldwyn's *My Foolish Heart* (1949) is a cumbersome weepie based on a short story by J. D. Salinger. Despite being scripted in the main by twins Julius J. and Philip G. Epstein (in Spike Jonze's *Adaptation*, 2002, ornery screenwriting guru Robert McKee, played by Brian Cox, declares their *Casablanca* the 'finest screenplay ever written'), *My Foolish Heart* garnered poor reviews and was soon forgotten. Nonetheless, *The Uninvited* yielded Young's instrumental theme tune, 'Stella by starlight', and *My Foolish Heart* offered a title song. Both became standards that have graced the modern jazz repertoire.

Once lyrics had been added by Washington, Harry James and His Orchestra popularized 'Stella by starlight' in 1947 with vocals by none other than a 32-year-old Frank Sinatra. It became a jazz tune with Charlie Parker in 1952, while Miles Davis, Chet Baker, and Bill Evans are among the many other jazz musicians to have covered it. In the 1960s, actor-singer Sergio Franchi featured it on television, and Ray Charles performed it in Martin Scorsese's 1995 gangster film *Casino*. One curious detail: as the title had to be incorporated into the lyrics, it appears as a phrase only once, about three-quarters of the way through the song.

The Oscar-nominated 'My foolish heart', dubbed by Margaret Mears in the movie for the actress Susan Hayward, lost out to 'Baby, it's cold outside' by Frank Loesser, an honourable defeat. The song took off in 1950 in hits for Sandy Evans with the Gordon Jenkins Orchestra and for Billy Eckstine, whose rendition sold over a million copies. As a jazz arrangement, tenor saxophonist Gene Ammons set the pace in 1950; within that decade, stirring versions by vocalist Carmen McRae and bassist Ray Brown solidified its reputation. (A tidbit for completists: though written in the key of G, Bill Evans and Tony Bennett duetted on it in B flat, while Sinatra opted for … A flat.)

The Polish-born émigré composer Bronislaw Kaper joined forces with Washington to create 'On Green Dolphin Street' (preposition 'on' added) as the title song to a 1947 MGM film starring Lana Turner and Van Heflin, which the eminent film critic Leslie Halliwell described as a 'silly nineteenth-century romance climaxed by rather a good earthquake'. None other than the 'Velvet Fog', Mel Tormé, sang it in the movie, though he did not have a hit with it. It is, like 'My foolish heart', a challenging song for a singer. Often performed instrumentally, this tale of lost love became a jazz standard courtesy of Miles Davis's muted trumpet on his album '58 Sessions, which also happened to include an interpretation of 'Stella by starlight'.

In the 1950s and early 1960s, Washington collaborated frequently with composer Dimitri Tiomkin, with whom he had as fruitful a relationship as he had earlier with Victor Young. Washington and Tiomkin received Oscar nominations for 'Blue Pacific blues' from Miss Sadie Thompson (1953), 'The high and the mighty' (1954), 'Strange are the ways of love' from The Young Land (1957), 'Wild is the wind' (1957), and 'Circus world' (1964). One of the best-known of his theme songs from this period is for the Anthony Mann-directed Western starring James Stewart, The Man from Laramie (1955), composed with Lester Lee, and put in the charts by Al Martino. It did even better in Great Britain where, as I well remember from my own childhood, Jimmy Young had a number one hit with that memorable song.

Undoubtedly the most famous of these title songs is from the Western classic High Noon, Stanley Kramer's 1952 production for United Artists. This plaintive ballad, often known unofficially by its first line, 'Do not forsake me', won an Oscar for Washington and Tiomkin. Cowboy actor and Western singer Tex Ritter performs 'High noon' with unusually sparse instrumental accompaniment over the opening credits, and it is reprised vocally, also as a whistle, and with orchestral accompaniment during later scenes. The song's lyric, more complex than it at first seems, functions as an oblique narrational device. By establishing a distance between Ritter's voiceover and the character of Marshal Will Kane (Gary Cooper), the song expresses Kane's feelings as he faces the possible loss of his new wife Amy (Grace Kelly) in doing what he feels is his duty to confront outlaw Frank Miller (Ian MacDonald), who is returning to town on the midday train. But the song goes further by summarizing the plot obliquely and by foreshadowing its resolution at the end of the film.

In 2003, writing in the journal *Senses of Cinema*, British film scholar Deborah Allison analyses the song's decisive influence on the growing popularity of the movie theme song during the 1950s. She pays particular attention to the way the song was cross-marketed between the record industry and film companies via the recording arms of Hollywood that emerged in the wake of the post-Second World War collapse of the studio system. 'High noon' could have ended up solely as a phonograph record. The decision to include it in the movie was only taken during postproduction, when Tiomkin felt the film badly needed a song. Ritter refused at first to record it, perhaps only too aware that it had already been a huge hit for Frankie Laine in a version with more generalized lyrics four months ahead of the film's premiere. In the event, Laine's rendition of the song boosted box-office returns for a film that had initially received a lukewarm response. Ned Washington, doubtless not to his displeasure, saw the line blurred between writing for films and for a modernized Tin Pan Alley now focused firmly on a synergistic relationship with cinema and later with television. Sensing new opportunities afforded by original dramatic productions in television, Washington and Tiomkin wrote the theme song for *Rawhide* (1959), which ran until 1965 on CBS and remains one of the finest Western series, one that introduced a young Clint Eastwood to the viewing public as the character Rowdy Yates. Sung by Frankie Laine, the ballad delivers an infectious refrain plus two perfect hooks in the form of a cracking whip.

Losing out in an Oscar race to Henry Mancini and Johnny Mercer's 'Moon river' is no disgrace; it happened to 'Town without pity', which Washington and Tiomkin wrote as the title song for a United Artists 1961 movie about a rape trial of American GIs stationed in Germany. But when UA's sister division Musicor brought in a young producer named Phil Spector and a rising pop balladeer named Gene Pitney to record the song, Washington was incensed by the radical arrangement of his song to suit Pitney's emotive style. Nonetheless, it was the first of many hits for Pitney; following its success, Paramount hired him to perform the title song, written by Burt Bacharach and Hal David, to John Ford's 1962 Western classic *The Man Who Shot Liberty Valance*. As with 'High noon' nine years earlier, 'Town without pity' helped the eponymous movie to click at the box office after its very slow start.

Washington's career began its ride into the sunset in the 1960s, at a time when the singer-songwriter phenomenon emerged (Bob Dylan, another great Jewish songwriter, set the tone) and when pop and rock bands started to write their own material (John Lennon and Paul McCartney were the standard-bearers). Though traditional songwriting teams continued to produce hits, they were slowly being overtaken by performers themselves – and in the case, for instance, of Carole King (one half of a brilliant writing partnership with Gerry Goffin), as a million-selling recording artist herself.

Though he continued to work on films until 1973, Washington died on 26 December 1976 in Beverly Hills, California, aged 75. His career had spanned vaudeville, Tin Pan Alley, Broadway, Hollywood, and television. He had worked with some of the finest composers of popular music: Victor Young, Dimitri Tiomkin, Leigh Harline, Lester Lee, Max Steiner, Hoagy Carmichael, Allie Wrubel, Sammy Stept, Michael Cleary, George Duning, Jimmy McHugh, Bronislaw Kaper, and Walter Jurmann. He has a place in the National Academy of Popular Music Songwriters' Hall of Fame, and from 1954 to 1976 served as vice-president of the American Society of Composers, Authors, and Publishers (ASCAP), in which capacity he crisscrossed the country regularly by train, as he disliked flying.

By all accounts, Washington handled his measure of celebrity modestly, and he is remembered as genial, generous, and ever gentlemanly in a generally cut-throat business. A speedy writer, who could complete a song in one day, he was also smart enough to sit on the finished article until publishers' contract renegotiation time came around. In *A Fine Romance*, his witty and erudite book on Jewish composers of the Great American Songbook, David Lehman recounts Sammy Cahn's reply – 'the money' or 'the phone call' – to the burning question to songwriters of which came first, the words or the music. But in line with the conventional practice among songwriters, Washington preferred to find words to match a composer's musical ideas rather than present lyrics alone and upfront (Oscar Hammerstein proved the exception to this rule in his work with Richard Rodgers). Ira Gershwin neatly described the process as 'fitting words mosaically to music already composed'.

Ned Washington contributed to over 100 movies (including forty title songs) and won three Academy Awards out of twelve nominations in all, which score puts him fifth among lyricists after Cahn, Mercer, Paul Francis Webster, and the team of Marilyn and Alan Bergman. He might have been excused had he chosen to alter gleefully the title of his own composition: 'Hi-diddle-dee-dee (a *lyricist's* life for me)'.

Index

Note: literary works of authors who are chapter subjects are listed at the end of their personal entries; other literary works are generally not indexed.

A

Achebe, Chinua, 71–2, 73, 76
Alexander, Sidney, 102
Allison, Deborah, 120
Altman, Rick, 114
Alun-Jones, Deborah, 43
Amvrosija, Sister/Mother, 40–1
Antoine, André, 10, 11
Arendt, Hannah, 37
Arnold, Matthew, 8
Attlee, Clement, 105
Auden, W. H., 67
Austin, Sarah, 46

B

Barker, Elspeth, 67–8
Barker, George, 61–2
  literary reputation, 66–7, 69
  portrait, 60
  works: *Anno Domini*, 61; *Calamiterror*, 61; *Collected Poems*, 69; *Poems*, 66; *The True Confession of George Barker, Book One*, 61; *The View from a Blind I*, 67
Barker, Raffaella, 68
Barker, Sebastian, 68
Barry, Tina, 104
Baudelaire, Charles, 15
Bayley, John, 69
Beckett, Samuel, 75
Belgium
  French perceptions of, 15
  see also Brussels, Ghent
Betjeman, John, 50, 105
Bjørnvig, Thorkild, 36
Blixen, Karen, 31–8
  celebrity friends and visitors, 33, 35
  portrait, 32
  radio talks, 36–7
  use of pseudonyms, 33, 35
  works: journalism and magazine work, 37; *Anecdotes of Destiny*, 37; *Last Tales*, 37; *Out of Africa* [*The African Farm*], 34–5; *Seven Gothic Tales*, 33; *Shadows in the Grass*, 37; *The Angelic Avengers*, 35, 37; *Winter's Tales*, 36

Bloom, Ken, 115
Bloor, Robert Henry Underwood, 108
Boorstin, Daniel, 2
Booton, Norfolk, 43–4
  post office, 44
  St Michael the Archangel church, 48–50
Borrow, George, 45
Borum, Poul, 34
Bourdieu, Pierre, 5
Braudy, Leo, 4, 5, 7
Briggs, Asa, 44
Brussels
  Avenue Maurice Maeterlinck, **xii**
  Chambre des Imagiers, La, 2
Burrow, Edward J., 106–7
Buysse, Cyriel, 6
Byron, Lord, 3

C

Carlyle, Thomas, 46
Carpenter, Maurice, 68
Castellanos, Rosario, 88, 89–90, 93–5
  portrait, 95
  works: essays, 89, 94; *An Attempt at Self-Criticism*, 94; *Book of Lamentations* [*Officia de tinieblas*], 94; *Ciudad Real*, 94; 'Death of the tiger', 93–5
celebrity
  and the commercialized literary system, 3
  but not celebrity author, 31
  definitions of, 2
  origins of, 3
  promoted by authors, 7
  studies, 2–3, 5
  and television, 53
  vs literary reputation, 3–4
Chadwick, Owen, 48
Chagall, Marc, 98, 100–2
Chagall, Vava (Brodsky), 102
Chignell, Thomas William, 108
Churchill, Winston S., 87
Coburn, Alvin Langdon, 11, 13
Conrad, Joseph, 5
Courthorpe, William John, 47
Cox, C. B., 63
Crosby, Bing, 116
Currey, James, 73

D

Dahon, Renée, 13, 21–8

Danish writers and literary circles, 34, 36
Darwin, Charles, 20
Debussy, Claude, 10, 16–18
Dennison, Matthew, 55
Dinesen, Wilhelm, 31–2
Dinesen, Isak *see* Blixen, Karen
Dorsey, Tommy, 116
du Maurier, Daphne, 35
Duhamel, Georges, 18
Dylan, Bob, 63, 120

E
Eggers, Dave, 7
Eliot, T. S., 59, 61, 66
Elwin, Frances, 43–4, 46
Elwin, Whitwell, 42–52
  articles written, 44, 45
  as biographer, 48
  and Booton Church, 48–50
  as editor of *Quarterly Review*, 43–7
  as editor of volumes of poems and letter, 47–8
  female friends, 50–1
  as manuscript reader, 47
  portrait, 42, 51
  sons, 51–2
  visitors to, 47
Emerson, Ralph Waldo, 16

F
Fabre, Jean-Henri, 14
Feast, Willis, 52
Finch-Hatton, Denys, 33
Ford, John, 13
Forster, John, 45, 48–9
Fort, Paul, 10
Fraser, Robert, 67, 69
Fry, Stephen, 52

G
gardener-authors, 56
George, Stefan, 10
Ghent, Collège Sainte-Barbe, 8
Gide, André, 16
Gillès, Daniel, 38
Gissing, George, 3
Glass, Lauren, 4–5, 6–7
Glendinning, Victoria, 55, 58
Goldwyn, Samuel, 1, 25
Gourmont, René, 16
Graves, Robert, 66
Grønkjær, Pernille Rose, 38, 40

H
Haggard, H. Rider, 97
Haggard, Stephen, 97–9
Haggard, Virginia, 96–104
  family and famous friends, 97–8
  as photographer, 102–3
  portrait, 96
  works: *Groeselenberg Diaries 1970–1997*, 103; *Lifeline*, 98, 103; *My Life with Chagall*, 98, 103; *The Spare Room*, 103
Hampton, Christopher, 25
Hanse, Joseph, 28
Harrison, Robert Pogue, 57
Hemingway, Ernest, 6, 7, 38
Heretica, 36
Hesbjerg Castle, 31, 38–41
High Falls, New York, 100–1. 103–4
High Noon, 119–20
Hill, Geoffrey, 72
Hughes, Langston, 71
Hull, Tristram, 68
Hurston, Zora Neale, 4

I
Ishiguro, Kazuo, 75
Itteringham, Norfolk, 68

J
James, Henry, 5
Jeffares, A. Norman (Derry), 73
Jekyll, Gertrude, 56
Jeune Belgique, La, 9
Jones, Eldred Durosimi, 74
Journal of Commonwealth Literature, 73

K
Kettle, Arnold, 72

L
Lambersy, Werner, 2
Langbaum, Robert, 34
Langlands (Barker), Elspeth, 67
Le Roy, Grégoire, 8, 9
Leblanc, Georgette, 6, 13–14, 16, 17–23, 26, 27
Lee, Harper, 7
Leeds, 71–3
Lehman, David, 121
Leirens, Charles, 101–2
Lemaître, Jules, 16
Lemonnier, Camille, 9
Lennon, John, 63

Lethem, Roland, 2
Lewis, Matthew, 87
Lewis, Simon, 34
literary criticism
    in the 19th century, 45–6
    by journalists vs academics, 8, 46
literary culture
    autonomous vs heteronomous, 5
    US vs European, 4
literary figures holding public office, 87–8
Lockhart, John Gibson, 44–5
Lockwood, Sebastian, 68
Losh, Sarah, 43, 48–9
Lugné-Poe, Aurélien, 10, 11, 18
Lutyens, Edwin, 51, 56
Lytton, Emily, 51

M
Maeterlinck, Maurice, 1–30
    ambiguously viewed in France, 19
    athleticism of, 6
    aversion to prizes and titles, 10, 22–3
    celebrated school colleagues, 8–9
    considerable fame of, 1, 16, 29–30
    education, 8–9
    host of *Fêtes Bleues*, 20
    Hollywood involvement, 1, 25
    homes, 13–14, 19, 20, 23, 26
    influences on, 13, 16
    as naturalist, 14, 17
    'no time for acting', 12
    partner/wife *see* Dahon, Renée; Leblanc,
        Georgette
    in Paris, 9–11, 13
    plagiarism accusations, 29
    political attitudes, 22
    portrait of, 11
    publishers of, 9, 10
    recent reassessments of, 29
    as reluctant celebrity, 4–6, 20, 22
    response of reviewers, 14–15
    street named after, **xii**
    and Symbolism, 5, 10–13
    visits to United States, 1, 24–5, 27–8
    visual collaborators, 13
    work neglected post 1949, 1
    works: early poetry, 9; film scripts, 25; jour-
        nalism, 28; nature essays, 16–17; *Aglavaine
        and Selysette*, 13; *Alladine and Palomides*, 12;
        Annabella, 13; *Ariane and Bluebeard*, 19;
        Blue Bubbles, 1, 28; *Death [Our Eternity]*,
        23; *Hothouses*, 5, 9, 26; *Interior*, 12;
        Joyzelle, 19; *Monna Vanna*, 18; *Pelleas and
        Melisande*, 10–11, 16–18, 20 (opera, 10,

16, 17–18, 28); *Princess Isabelle*, 27; *Princess
        Maleine*, 1, 8, 9–10, 15; *Sister Beatrice*,
        19; *The Blind*, 10; *The Blue Bird*, 1, 2, 16,
        21 (films of, 21–2; opera, 24); *The Buried
        Temple*, 19; *The Death of Tintagalies*, 12;
        The Double Garden, 19; *The Glass Spider*,
        27; *The Great Secret*, 26; *The Intelligence of
        Flowers*, 2, 19–20; *The Intruder*, 10; *The
        Life of Ants*, 26–7; *The Life of the Bee*, 1,
        14, 16–17; *The Life of Space*, 26; *The Life of
        Termites*, 26, 29; *The Mayor of Stilemonde*,
        23, 27; *The Miracle of St Anthony*, 19, 27;
        The Seven Princesses, 10, 12; *The Treasure
        of the Humble*, 12, 13, 14; *Twelve [Fifteen]
        Songs*, 13, 26; *Wisdom and Destiny*, 14, 16
Mahony, Patrick, 8, 18
Mallarmé, Stéphane, 9–10, 13, 15–16
Malraux, André, 88
Manning, Olivia, 99
Marais, Eugène, 29
Marx Brothers, 117
Mathias, Roland, 63
McCarthy, Cormac, 7
McNeil, John, 98–100
Melville, Herman, 4
Mexico, 90, 93
Middleton, C. H., 58
Miller, Jason, 114
Milton, John, 87
Minne, Georges, 9
Minns, James, 50
Mirbeau, Octave, 1, 8–10, 15
Mole, Tom, 3
Monastery, The, 38, 40–1
Mortier, Roland, 18
movies, music for, 114–21

N
Nettlefold, J. K., 105–11
    portrait, 106
    works: *From a Country Rectory*, 105, 108–9;
        Unusual Partners, 105, 108
Neville, Derek, 68
Ngugi wa Thiong'o, 70–8
    arrest and imprisonment, 74–5
    as journalist, 71
    in Kenya, 74–5, 77
    portrait, 70
    in the UK, 71–3
    writing in Gikuyu, 74
    works: memoirs, 76; *A Grain of Wheat*, 71;
        Decolonizing the Mind, 76; *Detained: A
        Writer's Prison Diary*, 75; *Devil on the Cross*,

75; *Globalectics*, 76; *Homecomings*, 74; *I Will Marry When I Want*, 74; *Matigari*, 72; *Moving the Centre*, 76; *Penpoints, Gunpoints, and Dreams*, 76; *Petals of Blood*, 74; *The River Between*, 71; *Weep Not, Child*, 71, 73; *Wizard of the Crow*, 76

Nicolson, Harold, 53, 55, 56
Nicolson, Nigel, 55, 56
Nietzsche, Friedrich, 16
Nobel Prizes, 75–8
  Churchill's, 87
  Dylan's, 75
  Faulkner's, 28
  Hemingway's, 6
  Maeterlinck's, 1, 22
  Paz's, 88
Norch, 68
Norfolk (UK) churches, 48–50
Norwich, 109–10
  Bristow's Paperbacks, 68
  Octagon Chapel, 109–10
Novalis (Georg Philipp Friedrich Freiherr von Hardenberg), 13
Nwaubani, Adaobi Tricia, 77–8

O
Ortega, Daniel, 88

P
Paris, Bouffes-Parisiens, 11
Parton Street poets, 62
Paz, Octavio, 88–9
  portrait, 91
  works: 'Obsidian butterfly' (*Mariposa obsidiana*), 90–3, *Poetry, Myth, Revolution*, 89; *Sun–Stone* [*Piedra de sol*], 88; *The Labyrinth of Solitude*, 90–2, 93
Peake, A. S., 109
Pevsner, Nikolaus, 49
Pinocchio, 117–18
Pocahontas, 44
Pope, Alexander, 47–8
Popma, Rachel, 88
Pugin, Augustus, 49
Pynchon, Thomas, 7

Q
Quarterly Review, 43–7

R
Reeve, Henry, 44
Retté, Adolphe, 15
Rodenbach, Georges, 2, 8, 9

Rolfe, John, 44
Roth, Philip, 7
Rushdie, Salman, 77
Ruskin, John, 20, 49
Russell, Sheridan, 24–5

S
Sackville-West, Vita, 53–9
  as gardener, 53, 56–7
  as journalist, 56
  as novelist, 57
  as poet, 55–6, 57, 58–9
  portrait, 54
  radio talks, 58
  works: gardening books, 56; *All Passion Spent*, 58; *Chatterton*, 57; *Country Notes*, 56; *Family History*, 58; *Grand Canyon*, 58; *Heritage*, 57; *Seducers in Ecuador*, 57; *The Dark Island*, 58; *The Dragon in Shallow Waters*, 57; *The Edwardians*, 58; *The Garden*, 58; *The Land*, 58
Salisbury, Mollie, 53
Schickel, Richard, 3
Scranton, Pennsylvania, literary figures from, 114
Sebald, W. G., 81
Senior, Olive, 88
Seymour, John, 79–86
  portrait, 80
  views on Africa, 81–3
  views on conservation, 84–5
  works: travel guides, 80–1; *Blessed Isle*, 85–6; *England Revisited*, 84; *I'm a Stranger Here Myself*, 84; *One Man's Africa*, 81–2; *Retrieved from the Future*, 79; *The Companion Guide to East Anglia*, 80–1; *The Complete Book of Self-Sufficiency*, 79, 83–4; *The Fat of the Land*, 79–80, 83; *The Hard Way to India*, 81
Seymour, Sally, 83
Shapiro, Karl, 62
Shephard, Alex, 75
Short, Robert, 2
Sissinghurst Castle, 53, 57
Sitwell, Edith, 58
Sitwell, Osbert, 58
Smart, Elizabeth, 68
Snow, C. P., 17
Sondheim, Stephen, 113
songwriting, 113–15
Soyinka, Wole, 71, 76, 77
Stand, 73
Stein, Gertrude, 5, 7

Storck, Henri, 102–3
Swansea, 64
Symbolism/Symbolists, 9–13
    poets, 13

T
Théatre Libre, 11
Thomas, Dylan, 61–6
  portrait, 65
  posthumous reputation, 66
  works: *18 Poems*, 64; *25 Poems*, 64; *A Child's*
    Christmas in Wales, 63; *A Visit to America*,
    64; *Collected Poems*, 64; *Deaths and*
    Entrances, 64; *Portrait of the Artist as a Young*
    Dog, 64; *Reminiscences of Childhood*, 63, 64;
    Return Journey, 63; *Under Milk Wood*, 63,
    65–6; *Welsh Poets*, 63
Thurman, Judith, 35
Thwaite, Anthony, 62
'tie-ins', 18, 21
Tiomkin, Dimitri, 119

U
Uglow, Jenny, 43

V
Van Lerberghe, Charles, 8–9
Van Melle, Louis, 9
Van Reybrouck, David, 29
van Ruusbroec, Jan, 10
Verdi, Giuseppe, 87
Verhaeren, Emile, 2, 8, 10, 12, 22
Vig, Jørgen Laursen, 38–40 (portrait, **39**)

Villiers de l'Isle-Adam, Philippe, 9
von Blixen-Feineke, Bror, 32–3
Von Bosse, Alexandra Mary, 105, 108, 110–11
Vonnegut, Kurt, 7

W
Wain, John, 66
Wali, Obi, 71
Walker, Alice, 4
Waller, Max, 9
Waller, Philip, 5
Washington, Ned, 112–21
  Academy Awards, 118, 119
  portrait, 112
  songs of, 116–20
Watt, Margaret, 43
Wellek, René, 8
Wharton, Edith, 56–7
Whitcomb, Ian, 114
Wilder, Thornton, 17
Williams, Hank, 64
Wolfe, Tom, 7
Woodforde, James, 43
Woolf, Virginia, 57, 58, 59

Y
Yeats, W. B., 66
York, Lorraine, 5
Young, Victor, 116, 118

Z
Zinsser, William, 113